Walk!

Lanzarote

with

Jan Kostura and
David & Ros Brawn

DISCOVERY WALKING GUIDES LTD

Walk! Lanzarote
First Edition - June 2004
Second Edition - July 2009
Third Edition - August 2012
Fourth Edition - September 2017

Copyright © 2017

Published by
Discovery Walking Guides Ltd
10 Tennyson Close, Northampton NN5 7HJ,
England

Maps
Maps are adapted from Lanzarote Tour & Trail Map
published by **Discovery Walking Guides Ltd**

Photographs
All photographs in this book were taken by the
authors.

Front Cover Photographs
39 Salinas del Río   **28 Caldera Blanca**

11 Salinas del Janubio   **13 & 14 GR 131**

ISBN 9781782750413

Text and photographs* © Jan Kostura,David
Brawn & Ros Brawn

Walk! Lanzarote
CONTENTS

The easy answer is loads! Starting with the **GR131** whose manicured trail winds its way diagonally across the island from **Playa Blanca** (SW) for 70 signed and wayposted kilometres before reaching **Órzola** (NE).

waypost marker

The full route of this Gran Recorrido, GR, is highlighted on the Lanzarote Tour & Trail Super-Durable Map. Usually split into five hiking days, fit mountain bikers see this as a 'one day challenge' to complete. Thanks to the **GR131** we have a new route, Walk 13 **Playa Blanca – Las Breñas – Yaiza GR131**, crossing the **Rubicón** to **Las Breñas** – two 5* refreshment stops to choose from – followed by an easy finish into **Yaiza** to catch a bus back to our start point; that easy finish also tidying up our Walk 14 finish route. **GR131** is a welcome addition to Lanzarote's resources but it is all linear, with few bus links, so getting back to your start can be problematical.

Down in the South Jan has pioneered an extension to our 'Playa del Pozo' route, Walk 22, to a surprise '**Secret Garden**' quite literally in the middle of nowhere. This surprise alone justifies a new route but he has also linked to our 'Femés – Playa Blanca' route, Walk 20, so that we now have a 'coastal' route to **Playa Blanca**; our routes will now take you all the way from **Arrecife** to the southern resort if you have a mind for a really big adventure.

'Secret Garden'

Walk 11 **Salinas de Janubio** is an easy stroll in this unique setting after which you can enjoy refreshments on the café terrace overlooking the salt pans.

mapboard at start of El Golfo Circular

Round the corner Jan has researched the new Walk 24 **El Golfo Circular**, a note in the previous Walk! Lanzarote. You can enjoy this adventure using Walk 24's detailed description and map or take a leisurely guided ramble organised by the Timanfaya Visitors Centre. With the new route established we have changed our Walk 25 'Between 2 Seas' to finish in **El Golfo** with its choice of cafes and restaurants, a more fitting conclusion than ending on the LZ-704 out in the country.

Montaña Blanca (Walk 7) is a completely new adventure in the centre of the island including one of the best examples of *Maretas*, carved underground water storage, on Lanzarote. In the popular Yaiza/Uga region Jan has produced a new circular route taking in a section of the **GR131** through impressive lava flows and taking in the extensive views from the ruined *Molino* in an easily accessed adventure – Walk 15.

Head north and we have some small changes to our classic **Montaña Cuervo** (Walk 26) for the changed access from the official car park, while **Montaña Sóo** (Walk 31) is another completely new adventure boasting great experiences that reward us far beyond the exertions in this previously unknown area. Continuing north Jan has combined our **Barranco del Malpaso** and **Forgotten Trail** routes out of **Haría** into a circular adventure combining the best of both trails.

views on Helechos Circular

You would not expect the authorities to remove a big transmitter aerial, or move the village rubbish bins, but these two changes caused Jan to research a new approach to our **Tabayesco Circular** (Walk 37). Jan has also reshaped Walk 38 **Helechos Circular** adding to the views plus starting in **Guinate**, easier for car drivers.

It is not all good news in the north as we have found that Walk 40 **Corona's Northern Tour** crossed private land, though we did not know this, which has now had its access closed. Jan has rerouted the **Corona** *caldera* into an easy circular walk based on the church in **Yé**. Good news is that the **Yé Cultural Centre** has reopened to return to its 'must visit' status in this welcoming and very unusual café that should be on everyone's northern itinerary. To round up our northern adventures Jan takes us away from the **Mirador del Río** crowds on an easy route exploring the jaw-droppingly beautiful views available as we progress along the island's northern promontory.

Cultural Centre Yé

After university, **Jan Kostura** set off on his travels, living and working in various far-flung places inspired by his passion for stimulating multicultural environments. However, being a stressed out desk-jockey in a hectic consulting business turned out not to be his thing, so after two years slouching in a chair he swapped the office for the more liberating environment of the great outdoors.

He found his second home in the Canary Islands, where he fell in love with the ambiance, the warm-hearted people, the constant sun, the stunning mountains and flamboyant nature.

Jan is also co-author (with Charles Davis) of **Walk! La Palma** (3rd edition) and **Walk! La Gomera** (4th edition), plus **Walk! Tenerife** (3rd edition with David & Ros Brawn) published by Discovery Walking Guides Ltd.

Nowadays Jan works as a mountain guide, organizing hiking expeditions and adventure holidays, and writes articles on travelling.

David & Ros Brawn moved to southern Tenerife in 1988. Finding a large resort filled with 'lost' tourists their first project was to produce the first integrated street plan of Las Américas/Los Cristianos, current editions of which continue to provide the resort mapping that everyone uses. Discovering the resort hinterland resulted in the first 'Warm Island Walking Guides' for Tenerife, then La Gomera and so Discovery Walking Guides was born.

Almost three decades later, David & Ros have hundreds of books and maps to their credit. Having pioneered the use of GPS for walkers, they've surveyed and mapped to produce the 'Tour & Trail' series of maps, 'Walk!' books and the popular 'Bus & Touring' maps. Along the way David became a member of the British Cartographic Society including contributions to its Maplines magazine.

For a full list of destinations and publications see:
www.dwgwalking.co.uk

HISTORY

Lanzarote and Fuerteventura's first inhabitants were the *Majos* (or Mahos), the approximate equivalent of the *Guanches* in the western Canary Islands. It is thought that they led a relatively uneventful existence until 1402, when the Norman *conquistador* Jean de Bethencourt arrived, befriending the *Majo* leader and taking peaceful control of the island from a camp in **Rubicón**, soon passing power to his nephew Maciot, the founder of the island's original capital **Teguise**.

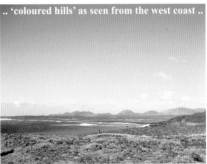

.. 'coloured hills' as seen from the west coast ..

The *Majos* named the island 'Titerroygatra', which translates as 'coloured hills', a name which would be just as appropriate today, though its current name is an adaptation of the name of an influential immigrant, Lancelotto Malocello.

GEOGRAPHY

Lanzarote is the most northerly and least mountainous of the Canary Islands, its highest point being 675 metres, **Peñas del Chache**, unfortunately taken over by the military and off limits to walkers. Its 169 kilometres of coastline varies between yellow and black beaches, cliffs and lava *malpaís*, offering some photogenic scenes. The island has been repeatedly shaped by volcanic activity, the most famous being the 1730-36 eruptions which formed **Timanfaya**, and the last in 1824 which created the volcanoes of **Tinguatón**, **Tao** and **Nuevo del Fuego**.

CLIMATE & AGRICULTURE

Lanzarote's close proximity to Africa is apparent in its weather. The dry, desert-like climate is interrupted by a few rainy days, typically in winter and early spring, but not amounting to much; for this reason the island's water supply comes from desalination plants. The modest height of Lanzarote's hills is insufficient to benefit from the humidity of the trade winds, but even so the lack of rain has not deterred the islanders from devising methods of growing a wide range of fruits and vegetables.

Particularly remarkable are the *zocos*, notably in **La Geria** where the black volcanic *picón* (ash) filters moisture to the roots and mulches the soil beneath, while keeping the plants cool. This is a windy island, and the agricultural plots are often protected from the prevailing winds by horseshoe shaped walls. When easterly winds blow they bring hot, dust-laden *calimas*, best avoided by staying indoors.

Ring 'o Roses

Lanzarote's pioneering approach to large scale outdoor art has been a resounding success. While other Canary Islands might paint up an old fishing boat to go on a new roundabout, this island does public art in the grand style. We like to feel that our own dictionary definition of these 'Thingys' has contributed.

1. Inanimate object that the speaker has temporarily forgotten the name of.
2. Large, or over large, man-made object of no discernible use prominently displayed in a public place, notably in the centre of large roundabouts. Associated with the Canary Island of Lanzarote and its most famous citizen César Manrique (artist, 1919-1992).

Dr Who Monster Thingy

César Manrique's legacy to Lanzarote is apparent in many aspects of the island's life, visibly in the squat white painted houses with green or blue window shutters but most notably in the 'sculptures' adorning roundabouts on the island's main roads.

Large Thingy in several parts

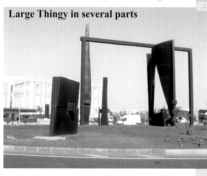

Sailing Thingy

Whether you consider these constructions as art seems open to question. Is the huge green tin-can cactus, outside the gardens in **Guatiza**, art or simply an advertisement in the same genre that American and Australian businesses use, equivalent to a giant 'hamburger' outside a burger bar?

Curvy Thingy

Some residents are defensive over these Thingys, believing that anything César Manrique promoted must be good for the island. You'll have plenty of opportunities to form your own Thingy opinion as you travel round.

Giant Key

Skinny Thingy

Egg Whisk and Planet

Nude Unicyling Thingy

When our 'Thingy' comments appeared in the first edition of this book we thought we might be deluged with complaints that we were being too flippant in our approach to the island's large scale art.

The reality is quite the reverse; we've been praised for making people think about the sculptures as unique pieces of art along with introducing 'Thingy' to the local language and encouraging the production of new Thingys.

FIRST IMPRESSIONS

If you are used to Mediterranean island destinations, or you've visited the western Canary Islands, your first arrival on the island might come as a bit of a shock. As your plane approaches the airport, you'll have an impression of barren starkness, relieved only by clusters and scatterings of cloned, squat white buildings, clustered thickly here and there on the coastline. But, give yourself a few hours to adapt, and you should begin to appreciate the subtleties of what is a chunk of African desert, overlain with volcanic spewings. The lava fields themselves have a certain weird beauty, and once you get over the withdrawal symptoms caused by the lack of trees, you'll find that Lanzarote is an island offering more colour and contrast than you might have assumed. The volcanic cones come in a variety of hues, and many parts of the coastline are dramatic and photogenic. Lanzarote might not appear at first glance to offer much variety or challenge for walkers; this book will change your opinion.

WHEN TO GO

If you want to walk, avoid the hot, dusty summer months of July, August and September. Be aware that, although Lanzarote has very little precipitation, you can hit some wet days; during our visits from February to April, there were four or five wet days. There were also a couple of *calimas*, the unpleasant hot, dust-laden east wind which picks up half the African deserts and then dumps it on the island. The skies darken with the suspended dust, and if you're a contact lens wearer or an asthma sufferer, you'll feel miserable. We wouldn't recommend walking in a *calima*, which can last anything from a couple of days to a week.

WHERE TO STAY

Almost all the accommodation is in the tourist resorts of **Costa Teguise**, **Puerto del Carmen** and **Playa Blanca**. The first two of these have the advantage of being close to the airport, having a reasonable bus service, and plenty of the usual tourist things, such as beaches, bars and shops. **Playa Blanca** is the place for you if you want to be near the ferry port for Fuerteventura, but it's a long way from everywhere else, and has a limited bus service. Sporting types can stay on the north coast at **Club La Santa** although there is not much distraction apart from within the complex itself.

GETTING AROUND THE ISLAND

There's bus information in the back of this book, but be aware that this can change. Check when you arrive, either at the Information Office which faces you as you emerge from the baggage hall at the airport, or in the resort tourist offices. Some routes operate only on work days, or only on Sundays (market specials), and some towns and villages have only three or four buses a day. If you intend to use buses to access and return from walks, check the times first, and be prepared to use taxis.

Easiest is to hire a car, easily available and at reasonable rates. When using a car for linear walking routes, try to link up with like-minded walkers with another hire car and use the 2CSK method. If you need a taxi when you are not near a tourist resort, ask in a bar and they will usually phone for you - but do buy a drink as well.

CÉSAR MANRIQUE

Within hours of the visitor's first arrival on Lanzarote, the influence of César Manrique (1919 - 1992) will already be obvious. The plain white, low-level buildings in traditional, unadorned style with their dark green doors and windows, and the sometimes startling sculptures that form traffic roundabouts, all bear witness to the singular effect this individual had - and still has - on the development of the island. Under his guidance, the **Jameos del Agua** caves were turned into a tourist attraction and an underground theatre. He was also the force behind the **Jardín de Cactus**, which although it contains the real thing, is oddly marked by an outrageously fake giant cactus in its car park. He had more than a hand in many other projects on the island, including the **Mirador del Río**, and the **Restaurante El Diablo** inside the **Montañas del Fuego** where volcanic energy is used to cook the food.

His main residence was **Taro de Tahíche**, north of **Arrecife**, now the **Fundación César Manrique**, since his surreal death in a road traffic accident in 1992 on the very roundabout that he had alerted the authorities to as dangerous. His vision continues under the auspices of the El Guincho environmental group. In 1993, UNESCO recognised his efforts in preserving the natural environment of the island by declaring the entire island a World Biosphere Reserve.

PARQUE NACIONAL DE TIMANFAYA

An incredible eruption of cataclysmic proportions and lasting six years began on 1 September 1730. Centred in the south of the island, the **Montañas del Fuego** or Mountains of Fire, caused devastation to an area of 200 sq. km. The ground is still hot to the touch in places, and a party trick by the guides is to toss a dry bush into a crevasse whereupon it is instantly consumed by fire. The feeling is that the boiling molten magma is still close enough for discomfort. The **Restaurante El Diablo** built on the **Islote de Hilarío** area within the park, uses the power of the volcano to barbecue the food, though it tastes no different to other forms of cooking and you do pay extra for this novelty.

Access to the park is restricted to cars and tour coaches (entrance fee payable), although there are guided walks available. If you would like to join one of these, apply at the **Centro de Visitantes** (Visitors' Centre) on the LZ-67 road, south of **Mancha Blanca**, in person or by phone on 928 840839. See Walk 23 'Termesana Guided Walk' for details. There's a tougher Walk 24 'El Golfo Circular' lasting about four hours and covering a distance of 8 kilometres which is arranged according to demand.

You can also take a coach tour from the parking area, taking in the weird volcanic landscapes, though you might find the multi-lingual commentary and taped music which accompany the tour irritating, and it is frustrating not to have the freedom to walk independently in these unique surroundings.

LANZAROTE'S SALT

Lanzarote produces about one third of the salt it needs, but the industry is not as important as it once was. The **Salinas del Río**, (see Walk 39 'Salinas del Río') almost on the island's most north-westerly point, are thought to have been constructed in the 15th century and are shown on maps drawn in 1590. The quantities produced here were more than sufficient to serve the island's needs; the excess was sold to La Palma and Tenerife.

Until 1775, these salt pans were the only ones on Lanzarote, but from that time on several were constructed to cash in on the growing market. **Salinas del Agujero** were constructed in 1940, near **Los Cocoteros** which, together with **Salinas del Janubio** are the principal remaining commercial salt pans The most scenic are **Salinas del Janubio** which exist thanks to the volcanic eruptions of 1730, when molten lava formed the walls of the natural lake of **Laguna de Janubio**. Salt production has declined in the last few decades; now the *salinas* are important havens for bird life.

Salinas del Janubio

Cactus farm near Guatiza

CACTI & COCHINEAL

Naturalised in all the Canary Islands, Prickly Pear cacti (opuntia) were introduced as a hedging plant whose edible fruits are collected by those prepared to risk being impaled on its sturdy spikes; you may see Canarians collecting these bright red or orange fruits with the aid of wooden tongs.

Prickly Pears also proved to be the most popular host plant for the cochineal beetle, which led to a thriving cottage industry in the valuable dark red dye harvested from these insects which are dried and ground. The development of artificial colourings almost killed the industry, but in recent years some manufacturers - especially of drinks, foodstuffs and cosmetics - have returned to this natural dye.

The cochineal beetles give away their presence by the protective white powder that they exude around themselves as they feed off the cactus sap. There are few naturalised cacti in the Canaries without a few of these telltale signs of infestation, and in a few villages including **Guatiza** and **Mala** they are still farmed despite the extremely labour-intensive nature of the industry, each tiny bug being collected by hand.

GOATS

Goats are survivors, living on a diet of tough, wizened and spiny plants at which any sheep would turn up its nose. Ideal livestock in this arid and unforgiving landscape, an estimated 15,000 or so live happily on what might appear to be barren desert. It would be easy to make the assumption that they are wild, but most have owners, as the presence of goatherds proves. Traditionally a source of meat, milk, cheese, wool, skins, tallow for candles and a host of herbal cures and remedies, the goat was historically an essential factor in the survival of Lanzarote's early settlers. These days there is a healthy market for goat's cheese and meat and a modest demand for crafts using goat's wool and skins. You would be unlucky not to see a herd of these multi-patterned creatures while walking on the island, and you'll probably envy them their sure-footedness and easy tackling of slippery slopes.

THINGS TO DO

If you want a change from walking (or the beach) there are several attractions to visit. The island's best natural wonders have been turned into profit making ventures, including the **Montañas del Fuego** inside the **Parque Nacional de Timanfaya**, the **Jardín de Cactus**, the **Mirador del Río**, the **Jameos del Agua**, a huge volcanic tube inside which is a lake, restaurant, bars and a theatre, and the **Cueva de los Verdes**, another part of the same massive volcanic tube which has been kept in a more natural state. There are several museums for anything from traditional and contemporary art, wine, agriculture, Lanzarote pirates and local crafts. There are boat trips for sightseeing, diving or fishing, or you could hop on the ferry to Fuerteventura from **Playa Blanca**, or see the tiny island of **La Graciosa**, reached by ferry from **Órzola** in about 25 minutes. Camel treks and horse riding are available, and the relatively flat terrain and quiet roads are ideal for cycling, with bicycle hire offered by several companies. **Costa Teguise** and **Puerto del Carmen** have golf courses.

Los Hervideros

Free attractions include the **Salinas del Janubio**, the coastline at **Los Hervideros** (the boiling springs), north of the salt pans where the sea boils and spouts through lava fissures. The jagged lava has been tamed into a series of narrow paths among the lava and

Charco de los Clicos

caves; if the sea is rough, expect to get a shower as the sea is forced up through natural blowholes. Also worth a visit is the half volcanic crater of **Charco de los Clicos** near **El Golfo**.

PLANT LIFE

Trees are scarce on Lanzarote, and where they do grow, it is thanks to careful planting and sustained watering. Some of the best plantings are in hotel gardens, where they provide a valuable mini-habitat for bird and insect life. Because the volcanic history of the island is still relatively recent, swathes of its surface are still littered with lava in one of its forms. These areas of *malpaís* show signs of the process of breaking down into smaller particles that will eventually become soil, as the colourful colonies of lichen prove. In other areas where volcanic ash rather than rock and lava streams covered them, (such as **La Geria**, Walks 29&30), fertile soil lies beneath black duvets of fine ash, which serve to protect the roots of Malvasia grape vines, figs and other crops while drawing moisture from the cooler night air, which then percolates downwards. This method of mulching with a thick layer of ash has been adopted for agriculture of all kinds often used with the horseshoe-shaped low walls or *zocos* which give additional protection from the prevailing winds.

The dampest part of Lanzarote, the north, has the deepest and most workable soil. The little town of **Haría** (The Forgotten Trail & Barranco del Malpaso and Circuit of Haría), sits in a fertile bowl where many types of fruit and vegetable crops are grown. The whole valley is dotted with Phoenix canariensis palms, and the roadsides are sparsely lined by white or pale pink Tamarix africana.

The Haría Valley

Look in the north of the island, especially around the **Risco de Famara** and **Haría** areas, for the island's own endemic miniature version of sea-lavender, Limonium puberulum. Easier to spot is the white *tajinaste*, Echium decaisnei which can reach 1½ metres in height, and the bright yellow dandelion-like Sonchus pinnatifidus. Another yellow giant is the fennel, Ferula lancerottensis, also an endemic. Mesembryanthemum crystallinum is a big name for the small, ground-hugging ice-plant which is common in many parts of the island, once used in the production of a type of soda.

2CSK - The Linear Solution

We've worked hard to ensure that our routes are as accessible as possible, though Lanzarote's landscape means that on our long linear routes and on the **GR131** we inevitably find ourselves a long way from our starting point. **2CSK** is our recommended solution to the problem of accessibility on linear routes. You need two walking couples/groups, each with its own hire car (2C).

- Get together and agree which linear routes you'll walk and when.
- On the day of the walk each group drives to one end of the linear route, locks the car, and starts walking the route.
- When the two groups meet, swap/exchange car keys (SK), and at the end of the walk drive the waiting hire car back to your agreed meeting point.

In practice, though, never underestimate the ability of the other group to become confused as to what they should be doing. You will only know if things have gone 'belly up' when you arrive at the end of that long route, having crossed with nobody, to find no car! However, when it works, it's a great way of seeing otherwise inaccessible regions of the island. The key to success is planning. Write everything down. Make sure both groups have a good map (Lanzarote Tour & Trail Map) and guide book. If you have mobiles, make sure each has the other's number. Write down the details of the other hire car and ask precisely where it has been parked when you meet.

Using GPS on Lanzarote

All the routes in Walk! Lanzarote are so accurately described that following our routes is simply a matter of following the walk description.
A GPS may not be necessary, but is useful if you want to know exactly where you are on a walking route, and also for finding the start of a route, especially if it's your first visit to the island. With the walking route's waypoints loaded in your GPS, simply activate the 'Go To' function for Waypoint 1. Mapping GPS units and 3G/4G phones running GPS apps give you a real time moving

map display. If you have the digital version of our Tour & Trail Map on your mapping GPS or phone, then you'll be able to see exactly where you are on all of our walking routes.

All the waypoints for Walk! Lanzarote walking routes are available as a free downloadable zip file. Download the zip file to your hard drive, unzip the file into its GPX, WPT and TXT folders for each waypoint file format. Then simply load the files you want into your GPS or phone app.

If you are thinking of a GPS for walking navigation then our book **GPS The Easy Way** is available as a free download inPDF format from our website.

Digital Custom Map editions of our Tour & Trail Maps are available from Discovery Walking Guides website. Special digital editions of Tour & Trail Maps are available for Viewranger and MyTrails apps; for more information see their websites.

Symbols Rating Guide

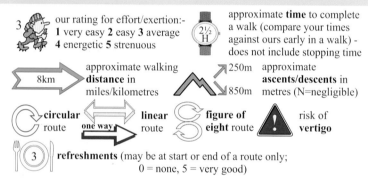

3 — our rating for effort/exertion:-
1 very easy **2** easy **3** average
4 energetic **5** strenuous

2½ H — approximate **time** to complete a walk (compare your times against ours early in a walk) - does not include stopping time

8km — approximate walking **distance** in miles/kilometres

250m / 850m — approximate **ascents/descents** in metres (N=negligible)

circular route   **linear** route (one way)   **figure of eight** route   risk of **vertigo**

3 — **refreshments** (may be at start or end of a route only; 0 = none, 5 = very good)

Walk descriptions include:
* timing in minutes, shown as (40M)
* compass directions, shown as (NW)
* heights in metres, shown as (1355m)
* GPS waypoints, shown as (Wp.3)

Notes on the text
Place names are shown in **bold text**, except where we refer to a written sign, when they are enclosed in single quotation marks. Local or unusual words are shown in *italics*, and are explained in the accompanying text.

A Note About Walking Times
Walking times create more discussion than any other aspect of walking guide books. Our walking times are for *continuous walking* at an easy pace without stops, representing the quickest time you are likely to complete a route. Most of us walk at a similar pace; approx 4-6kmh. As our routes are planned as fun adventures you are unlikely to simply march along the route from start to finish. We all take stops to enjoy the views, marvel at the flora, or simply to take a break. As a result, we suggest you add 25-50% to those continuous walking times, to allow for the stops you'll make along the route.

The map sections used in this book are taken from **Lanzarote Tour & Trail Super-Durable Map** and aligned so that north is at the top of the page. Waypoint positions and numbers refer to the walking route shown in that map section.

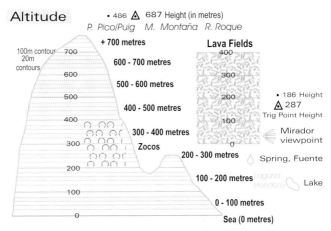

Altitude

• 486   △ 687 Height (in metres)
P. *Pico/Puig*   M. *Montaña*   R. *Roque*

100m contour
20m contours

+ 700 metres

600 - 700 metres

500 - 600 metres

400 - 500 metres

300 - 400 metres

Zocos

200 - 300 metres

100 - 200 metres   *Laguna Hondera*

0 - 100 metres

Sea (0 metres)

Lava Fields

• 186 Height
△ 287 Trig Point Height

Mirador viewpoint

Spring, Fuente

Lake

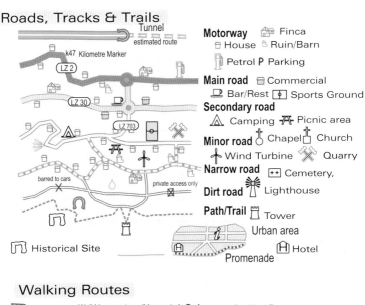

Roads, Tracks & Trails

Tunnel
estimated route

k47 Kilometre Marker

LZ 2

LZ 30

LZ 703

barred to cars

private access only

Historical Site

Motorway   Finca

House   Ruin/Barn

Petrol   P Parking

Main road   Commercial

Bar/Rest   Sports Ground

Secondary road

Camping   Picnic area

Minor road   Chapel   Church

Wind Turbine   Quarry

Narrow road   Cemetery,

Dirt road   Lighthouse

Path/Trail   Tower

Urban area

Promenade   Hotel

Walking Routes

Walk! Lanzarote walking route in **Red**

Combined Route

other trails in dashed grey

GR131

GR131

GR131 route outlined in **Green**

The Canary Islands lie approximately 100 kilometres west of North Africa's Atlantic Coast, and approximately 1100 kilometres south-west of the Spanish Mainland.

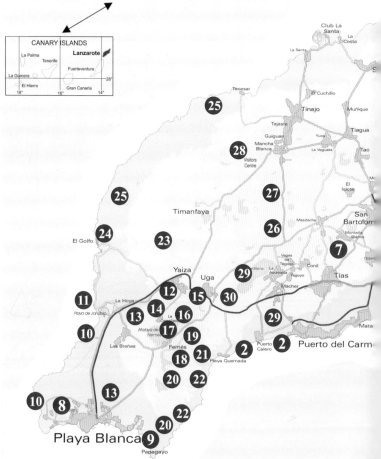

Remorseless sunshine combines with low humidity, and a barren rock/lava landscape covers much of the island. Protection against sunburn, sunstroke and dehydration should not be relaxed for even the easiest of routes.

BACKPACK A 25-30 litre day pack should easily cope with all you will need for a day's walking. We suggest a pack with plenty of outside pockets.

FOOTWEAR Whether you choose boots, shoes or sandals they must be up to the task. Whichever footwear you choose, do make sure that you've broken them in.

SUN PROTECTION Wear loose clothing and a comfortable sun hat that gives plenty of shade and stays on in windy conditions; 'Legionnaire' caps which protect neck and ears too. Use high-factor sun cream on all exposed skin and carry some in your pack for topping-up en-route. Wrap-round sunglasses protect eyes from UV radiation and grit. When you take a break, sit in the shade.

WATER & FOOD Dehydration is a real risk. Carry at least a couple of ½-litre water bottles add extra for longer, more strenuous routes. Even on short routes, carry survival rations; chocolate bars, dried fruit and the like provide welcome comfort when out in the wild.

MEDICAL KIT Take antiseptic wipes, antiseptic cream, plasters, bandage and lip salve. Include tweezers, and a whistle.

NAVIGATION Don't compromise - buy and carry the best guide book and the best map. A compass is useful to orientate yourself at the start of a route and for general directions, but a GPS is far more useful.

CLOTHING Choose loose comfortable clothing and add a lightweight, rainproof jacket to your back pack. The island might be mostly desert, but it does rain sometimes.

OTHER EQUIPMENT Digital camera, monocular (half the weight of a pair of binoculars), mobile phone, and money are recommended.

Safety

- Don't attempt high altitude routes in severe weather. Be prepared to abandon a route and turn back if bad weather closes in.
- Don't walk alone - or at least let someone know where you are planning to walk.
- Wear appropriate clothing and footwear, and carry the right equipment.
- Take frequent drinks of water.
- Shade is scarce on Lanzarote. Protect yourself from the sun.
- Start out early enough - allow plenty of time to complete the route before dark.
- Stay on the route. If it is impassable, retrace your steps.

Lanzarote's most popular easy walking and strolling route requiring no more than suitable footwear, clothing and sun protection. Beach side bars at **Playa Honda** mean you can conveniently stop for refreshment at the half way stage of the route. If you find 9+ kilometres of walking more than enough, your arrival in **Arrecife** close by the bus terminus makes it easy to catch a **Puerto del Carmen** bus back for your return.

'thingy' at Wp.2

We 'officially' start at **Matagorda** but you can begin anywhere along the promenade and pavements from the centre of **Puerto del Carmen**. From the **Hotel Faríones** simply add 5 kilometres and 75 minutes to our distance and times.

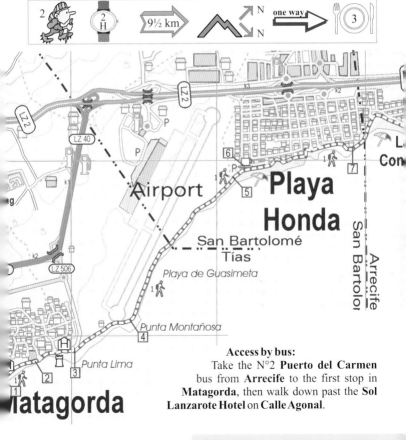

Access by bus:
Take the N°2 **Puerto del Carmen** bus from **Arrecife** to the first stop in **Matagorda**, then walk down past the **Sol Lanzarote Hotel** on **Calle Agonal**.

Access by car:
Calle Agonal, beside **Sol Lanzarote Hotel,** where we've always found plenty of on-street parking, even at weekends.

On foot from Puerto del Carmen: Simply walk down to the sea front and follow the beach-side pavement eastwards to meet our official start.

From **Calle Agonal** (Wp.1 0M) we follow the promenade (E) for an easy stroll to a rotating 'thingy' (Wp.2 6M). Next feature is a lava tower shortly before a grey rock 'thingy' set in a roundabout (Wp.3 12M). Now we leave tourism behind, past stone seats and an aerial-bedecked building before coming to the end of the runway (Wp.4 19M), the big jets making an impressive sight when taking off over us.

It's all easy strolling to pass the 'cozzie optional' small beach of **Playa de Guasimeta** before crossing a wooden bridge (Wp.5) to come onto the pebbledash slabs of **Playa Honda**'s promenade and the welcome sight of **Bar Mercedes** (Wp.6 44M) and **Bar Mesana** facing the beach.

Our promenade twists along beside the beach, passing a clutch of bars (Wp.7) before swinging left to round a crescent of sand. Our easy promenade stroll takes us past the beach and villas before turning inland to arrive at **El Cable Yacht Club** (Wp.8). Keeping straight ahead, we go right onto pebbledash slabs and then left to come onto the wide brick paved promenade for our final section into **Arrecife**.

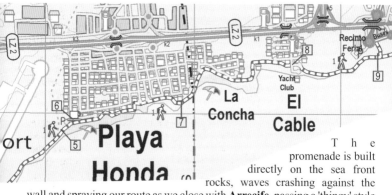

The promenade is built directly on the sea front rocks, waves crashing against the wall and spraying our route as we close with **Arrecife,** passing a 'thingy' style seating area. Passing an extensive car park and **Biosfera** centre on our left, the neo-classical *Cabildo* building comes into sight on our left along with a large rusty 'thingy'. An easy stroll brings us up to the start of the thematic park. At a 'muse' (Wp.9) we could short-cut left across the park to the bus station. Our full route goes on to the prow (Wp.10 95M) of the 'boat' theme park before swinging left around **Playa Reducto** to meet the road (Wp.11 100M), just to the right of the bus station.

Strolling round Arrecife's pedestrianised shopping streets is an entertaining experience so following the seafront road we pass the refurbished **Arrecife Gran Hotel** and yacht club before coming to the Tourist Information Office whose helpful staff can give a proper insight into the town's delights.

An adventure in two parts. First is an easy stroll along the clifftop promenade to **Puerto Calero** marina, followed by a cross country walk to the artisan style village of **Playa Quemada**; from where we can link with our southern adventures. Opt for the short version to the marina and then return on the water-bus (6€ single) and you have a family friendly day out. Continue on to **Playa Quemada** to get a feel for the real Lanzarote along with laid back village life.

2/3   3½ H   16 km*   100m / 100m   3

* 16kms to **Playa Quemada** and return

Access by bus: While we can return from **Puerto del Carmen** on the 25 bus service the Water-Bus (€6) from the marina back to the old port is the popular choice. There is no bus service for **Playa Quemada**.

From **Puerto del Carmen**'s old port (Wp.1 0M) we take the steps up by the **El Varadero Restaurant** to **Calle Los Infantes** which we follow to its end by the **Rincón Apartments**. We climb the rope-handrailed stair to come to the start of the coastal promenade (Wp.2).

Climbing the zigzag stair

It's an easy stroll passing the final villas to head out into the countryside. Navigation couldn't be simpler as we follow the broad path that runs along the top of the cliffs, before swinging inland to cross a rocky inlet (Wp.3). Our route runs out of the inlet into a flat barren landscape dotted with squat-walled villas as the path comes back to the cliffs before coming to the lava-walled gardens of villas at the entrance to **Barranco de Quiquere** (Wp.4 30M), a veritable oasis when set against this barren landscape.

Now we have a gentle stepped descent before crossing the watercourse followed by a steady climb; there's even a seat half way up if you want to take a break, plus a collection of stone seats just as we reach the crest beyond the last villa - now, how thoughtful is that?

If this is your first southern walk, allow yourself the luxury of taking in the distant views. Inland, the central massif finishes at the pass to **La Geria**, while the large building set on the final ridge is a *parapente* launch point. Depending on the winds, you might see whole flocks of these colourful fragile fliers gliding down to their landing strip inland from **Puerto Calero**.

Our broad path takes us along low cliffs set above a lava plateau foreshore before dropping into a small *barranco* and then climbing back onto the cliffs. We come up to overlook **Puerto Calero** marina at a path junction (Wp.5 54M); going right would take us up to the LZ-506 road and bus stop. We take the stone path descending into the *barranco* to cross the marina access road onto the **Paseo Marítimo**; the *paseo* climbs up to overlook the marina as we stroll along to its main entrance (Wp.6 61M).

Puerto Calero offers a selection of shops, cafes, bars and restaurants set against a backdrop of expensive nautical hardware; just the place for a leisurely break. The popular water-bus (€6) leaves from the marina for a stylish return to **Puerto del Carmen**.

The rock stairway before Wp.8

For our continuation on to **Playa Quemada**, we take the **Paseo Marítimo** (Wp.6 0M) from the marina entrance. Following the elegant walkway we pass the marina before turning inland up to a T-junction (Wp.7 10M) at the **Hotel Hesperia**.

Although it looks like a dead end, we go left (W) to walk past the restaurant entrance onto a small rock headland with marine rope railing.

We follow the rope down steps to cross a tiny artificial beach and climb a rock stairway that brings us up to the western end of the hotel from where we come inland beside the hotel to pick up a track (Wp.8) that curves up over the next headland.

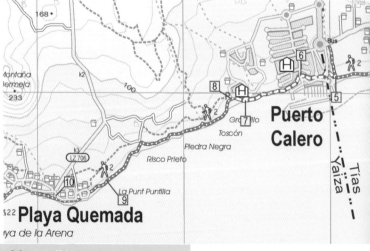

The dusty track takes us into an undulating landscape, quite adventurous compared to the manicured walkway to **Puerto Calero**. Staying on the track, we head towards the coast. This is another area used by quad bikers, resulting in a myriad of tracks and trails. To avoid confusion, keep to the coastal track/trail as we go through a series of gentle ascents and descents to head westwards across small hills and shallow valleys; when a track turns inland a walking trail links us to the next track section. Only when we walk up a longer than usual slope do we come into view of the first houses of **Playa Quemada**; this point (Wp.9) is grandly shown as a trig point of 22 metres on military maps, but is hardly noticeable on the ground.

Following the track, we come to the first houses, the track becoming tarmac for an easy stroll down the first street to a small square. Then it's downhill past the beach front houses to a restaurant (Wp.10 32M) where you could walk down the beach front instead of the road. Cutting through to the beach, we stroll along to the end of the houses to come onto the tarmac as it heads inland to the **7 Islas** and **La Casita** bar/restaurants.

As we sit on one of these terraces and take refreshment, we can absorb the charm of this informal settlement of small houses and weekender homes. Some might describe its rather disorganised style as scruffy, but there's no doubting its quaintness. Just as the track to **Puerto Calero** contrasts with the path to **Playa Quemada**, so does this settlement's casual approach contrast with the 'organised' development of the marina; in one short walk we've experienced three contrasting coastal settlements; just pick the one that seems most agreeable to yourself.

Take your time relaxing before returning to the resort by your outward route.

Costa Teguise's bold initiative to encourage discovering the resort by producing three walking routes has been popular. The overall route might be a bit contrived in places where trails have been constructed alongside pavements, but as a way to see the overall resort, both its seafront and its back side, it cannot be beaten. Another consequence of the official route is that previously abandoned areas of the resort have been cleaned up with some new gardens planted. If we have one criticism - it makes us feel quite mean to even have one - it is that once we leave the seafront, refreshment opportunities are non-existent so take water with you.

An official mapboard/streetplan

Pick up a streetplan from the Tourist Office and you are ready to go. The route's signs and signboards suffer from vandalism so our short hand notes and map section will prove useful in navigating our way round. It's unusual for us to not include timings along a route; however, as this is a strolling town walk with various options, they would serve no useful purpose in this case.

2   2-2½ H   12 km   60m / 60m   ↻   3*

* on seafront only.

Access from within Costa Teguise:
Simply walk from your accommodation to your nearest point on the walking route and start your adventure there.

Access by bus:
Route Nº1 runs between **Arrecife** and **Costa Teguise** (stops at **Las Caletas** in western **Costa Teguise** and **Hotel Salinas**, in the resort's east, plus 5 other locations in between) every 20 minutes for most of the day Mon-Fri and half-hourly for most of Sat/Sun/fiestas.

Access by car:
There is on-street car parking on the street accessing the western end of the promenade, plus extensive car parking on the inland side of the commercial centres facing **Playa Cucharas**.

Starting from the turning circle at the end of **Calle de los Volcanes** (Wp.1) we take the promenade (E) to meet the official red route (Wp.2) at a path junction; our return route on the full circular. Villas give way to the **Hotel Las Coronas** before we pass on to **Playa Bastián** where the green route joins the promenade (Wp.3) followed by walkways accessing the resort and a 'martello' tower lifeguard/red cross station for the beach.

At a pedestrian roundabout we keep right to follow the promenade past the **Blue Sea Beach Apartments** and a replica windmill overlooking **Playa Jabillo** (Wp.4). Round the beach, we pass the **Neptuno Commercial Centre** before coming to another replica windmill (Wp.5) opposite the **Apartamentos Nautilus**. Rounding the point we come in sight of the tall 'thingys' which dominate **Playa Cucharas**, the resort's main beach. As we cross the port's access road (Wp.6) we can take the short stroll along the dock to examine the thingys from close quarters.

Past a rusting thingy and Brit and Irish bars, we come to the head of the beach where walkways lead up to the parking areas. A collection of oversize plumbing parts on the seaward side of the promenade could possibly rank as a thingy as we traverse the main beach area to a junction (Wp.7) where a path leads left to the commercial centre while we continue right for the final section of the beach out to the breakwater (Wp.8).

Our route curves left to the breakwater protecting **Playa Los Charcos** where going left we follow the promenade around the beach and pass a replica windmill (Wp.9) and an inland lagoon which is part of **Sands Beach Villas**, then we're heading out into the country past an original windmill, dating from the sea salt era, to the end of the promenade (Wp.10) where we turn left following the 'red' route.

Heading inland on a dirt track, we come to the first of the contrived trails

(Wp.11) at the side of **Avenida de las Islas Canarias** which we follow to cross the **Ancones** dirt road before coming onto the pavement alongside a large roundabout (Wp.12).

Here the 'red' route goes SW on pavement marked by two wayposts before returning to a contrived trail at the third waypost (Wp.13) which parallels the pavement of **Avenida de las Palmeras** (SW) until we turn right at the next junction (Wp.14). We head along **Calle Atalaya** (NNW) towards **Hotel Beatriz** where, after a hundred metres, a dirt trail parallels the pavement. Pavement or trail, we head (NW) towards the expanding edifice of the hotel to where the road swings left for us to continue to a trail junction (Wp.15); here our Walk 5 comes down the trail to join us. Going left on the red route, we climb up a small escarpment to the graffitied ruin of a cottage, along with the remains of wayposts and notice board. The red trail then drops down to below road level in a picky descent before climbing beside the pavement to meet the road at the top of its gradient (Wp.16).

The trail at the resort's eastern edge

The section between Wp.15 & 16 is very contrived and we can skip the inconvenience of it by simply walking up the pavement, Walk 5, to the trail's continuation. A barren dry gully is piped under the road where we cross, the gully a surprising bright green 'river' of plant life, completely stuffed with Euphorbias on its far side of the road; unusual in these barren surroundings.

The 'green' ri

Taking the red trail, we arrive at a waypost alongside **Calle Chafari** (Wp.17) which we follow (N) until it crosses the street (Wp.18). Now we come down to cross a large dry watercourse, then gently ascend to the second feature of the official route, an old water cistern (Wp.19); the ruined cottage was the first feature. Leaving the cistern behind, we stroll down alongside the dry watercourse to a trail junction (Wp.20) where the blue and green official routes meet the red route.

Here you can shortcut back into the resort by following the blue and green route in reverse as it continues (SE) alongside the dry watercourse to cross **Calle La Laguna** and then on to a signboard on **Avenida de las Palmeras**. Here the official route goes left to a zebra crossing then continues as a trail heading alongside tourist developments (SE) to come onto **Avenida de las Islas Canarias** opposite the extensive car parking for **Centro Comercial Las Cucharas**.

From the junction (Wp.20), we take the combined route (SW) as our trail scales a small ridge before running down to cross **Calle Ruta del Norte**

(Wp.21) on a zebra crossing with signboards on each side of the road. Once again our manicured trail parallels the street, even turning right at the road junction to parallel **Calle de los Crotos**, before going right for a couple of metres for us to come onto the pavement just before **Residencial Las Gaviotas**. To find our trail's continuation we walk down the pavement (SW) to cross the street on a zebra crossing where we find the trail again (Wp.22).

Our trail drops down to cross the street just north of the road bridge and then climbs again to street level before coming to an unmarked junction (Wp.23) where we need to go left to cross a street before our route leads onto the pavement of **Avenida de las Palmeras** for us to walk along to a junction of the official routes (Wp.24).

From the official junction, the green (shortest) route heads left (SE) across the **Avenida de las Palmeras**, crossing **Avenida del Mar** before arriving on the seafront promenade at Wp.3 offering us a shortcut finish option.

Red/blue route goes right on a trail that crosses **Avenida del Golf** (Wp.25) for us to walk through tightly-packed villa developments on a concrete path. Keeping straight ahead (SW) we cross three small streets, plus a children's play area with seats, before emerging into the open on the trail's continuation for us to come down to **Avenida de Las Palmeras** again, which we cross on the zebra crossing (Wp.26).

Across the main road, we walk along the pavement towards the resort (E) to a waypost indicating our trail's continuation (Wp.27) through community gardens before crossing the **Avenida del Mar** on a zebra crossing. The gardens continue

Aloe vera between the villas

making for a picturesque stroll down to meet the seafront promenade (Wp.2). Now we simply turn right to retrace our outward route back to our start (Wp.1) at **Calle de los Volcanes**.

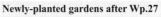

Newly-planted gardens after Wp.27

4 Sunday Market Special - Camino El Charco

With the advent of the car, many of Lanzarote's commerce routes were upgraded from donkey trails to tarmac roads. When Lanzarote was first colonised, pirate raids dictated establishing the capital at **Teguise**, protected by the **Castillo de Santa Bárbara**. From here routes ran down to the coast; one passing through the small settlement of **Teseguite** and then straight down to **Salinas El Charco**. Refrigeration largely killed the sea salt market, but this old donkey trail route is still shown on some maps. This is one old route which still survives, though the new **Tahiche-Mala** road necessitates a short diversion through a tunnel.

Sunday is the day to walk this route using a 'market special' bus, seeing the island's busiest street market before setting out on the old 'salt trail'.

Access by bus,
Sunday market specials go from **Costa Teguise** (Nº11), **Puerto del Carmen** (Nº12), **Arrecife** (Nº14)and **Playa Blanca** (Nº13).

Short Walk
To **Castillo de Santa Bárbara** and return, (ascents/descents 110 metres).

Our starting point is at the start of the access road to **Castillo de Santa Bárbara** (Wp.1 0M). If you are coming from the market, then make your way to the main road, cross over and walk up the pavement to reach our 'official' start. With the old castle above us we have a slogging ascent up the tarmac (SE) between storm-water eroded earth banks. As we ascend we are looking for a faint dirt track leaving the tarmac (Wp.2) which comes just before the

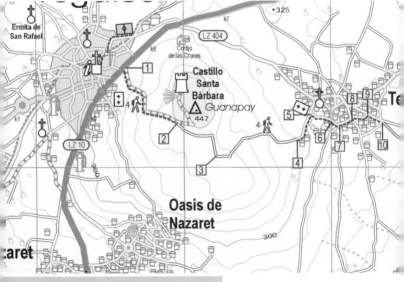

road gets even steeper. Gratefully, we leave the steepening tarmac to stroll along the narrow track between stone walls as it contours around the hill to come to cultivated fields contrasting with the generally barren landscape.

Views open up over **Teseguite** and down to the coast as our track goes right to go around another area of storm-water eroded earth banks.

...views open up over Teseguite ...

Keeping to the main track (Wp.3), we swing left towards **Teseguite** to stroll gently downhill with extensive views expanding over the valley and up to the **Ermita de las Nieves** and radomes of 'Capital Route - Haría to Teguise'. Our track swings downhill through the sunburnt landscape to bring us onto a tarmac street (Wp.4) and the first houses of **Teseguite**.

Teseguite might be a small settlement, but it can be confusing to navigate to find our exit route. Going left, we stroll down (NNE) to the second junction (Wp.5) marked by a 'palm tree' roundabout outside the cemetery, where we go right (E). We stroll gently downhill to cross over a village street, and pass **Casarino** on our right before coming to the next crossroads (Wp.6), where we go left (E).

It is downhill again to a T-junction (Wp.7) at the end of **Calle Revuelta**, where we go left and immediately right on **Calle Cadera** to come along to another T-junction (Wp.8). Here we go right to start our exit into the country. At a junction (Wp.9) with 'Finca Luna' signed left, we go right, and where the tarmac lane swings right, we go straight ahead on a dirt track (Wp.10), the

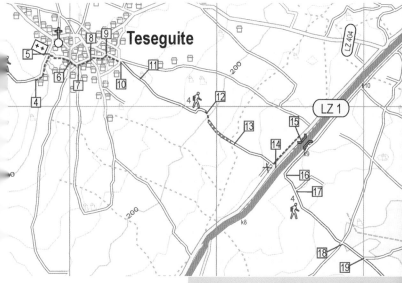

Camino El Charco - well, we did warn you it could be confusing.

We head out into the country between stone walls, passing a troglodyte style hut (Wp.11) to come into an area littered by a 'rain of stones'. It's downhill on the faint track, and after it swings left and right views open up across the sloping plain to **Montaña Corona** with **Costa Teguise** peeking round its base. Water erosion has washed away sections of the track as cultivated fields start on our left, just before the track runs out at a triangular field (Wp.12).

To find our onward route we go right across the edge of the field to go through a gap in a 'pile of stones' wall to find a faint trail heading down towards **Montaña Corona** along a gully. We pick our way down the shallow gully between fields to come out into the open; ahead a pair of cultivated fields stands out in the barren landscape. Keeping the water runoff on our right, we are back to easy strolling, our trail crossing the runoff (Wp.13) and becoming better defined as we come to the cultivated fields. Now we simply keep straight ahead on the track, passing a pylon and then a 'bedstead' gated property on our right where the track becomes more used, to come down to meet the old main road (Wp.14).

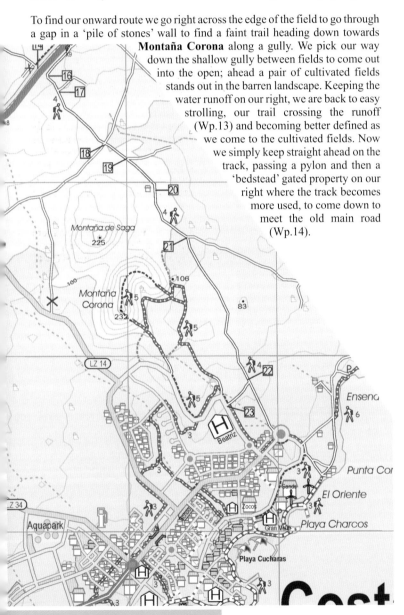

Originally our route went straight across the old main road, but the new LZ-1 road is wider, faster and busier. To avoid any risk we go left (NE) on the old road to a tunnel under the LZ-1 (Wp.15) where we come onto the remains of the old road. Going right, we continue alongside the new road on a track to come back to the line of the **Camino El Charco** (Wp.16). Obstacle passed, we are back to simple navigation as we follow a track heading towards **Montaña Corona** (SSE) and the coast, passing a minor track off to our left (Wp.17) and a pair of ruins before topping a rise where our track runs down to cultivated fields and a crossroads of tracks (Wp.18).

Coming down to the crossroads from the new road it is very noticeable how the land has changed. Above the main road the land is cheerfully barren, but below, it's as if this forgotten plain is cowering beneath the dominant heights of **Caldera** and **Tahíche**. Grey is the dominant colour, relieved a little by the spiny grey-green Lanzarote Fire Bush (Launaea arborescens) which dominates the long-abandoned fields in this harsh landscape.

At least it is easy walking, passing a minor track (Wp.19) as we come gently uphill past cultivated fields to the unexpected sight of a house. Passing the house (Wp.20) and then another track off left to a field, we walk alongside a stone wall to come over a small rise; views open up to the ocean, though **Costa Teguise** is hidden behind the bulk of **Montaña Corona**. We drop down to cross a water runoff (Wp.21) where a faint track goes straight ahead, while our track swings right.

It's a featureless *malpaís* littered with stones, our track changing to a more comfortable sand base as we curve towards **Costa Teguise**. An easy stroll brings us back onto the *malpaís* at a small rise which brings the sea and **Costa Teguise** into view.

Our track becomes fainter as we cross a small water runoff (Wp.22) and then come up to see our faint track running across towards the **Hotel Beatriz** reception. The track gets even rougher as we pick our way down to step gratefully onto the pavement (Wp.23) outside this large hotel. From here we can follow Walk 3, in either direction, or follow the pavements into the centre of the resort.

Approaching Costa Teguise

5 Montaña Corona

While **Playa Blanca** has its **Montaña Roja**, **Costa Teguise** has **Montaña Corona**. Although the peaks differ by only 30 metres altitude, their natures are quite different. **Corona** might only be 232 metres high, but it is quite a tricky peak with a steep, pathless, final ascent and a slippery, shale-covered path descent. These two sections are joined by a ridge top walk around the rim of the *caldera* which might upset vertigo sufferers, and certainly should not be attempted in windy weather.

Those are the bad points, but for experienced walkers the views from the top fully justify the difficult ascent, and the ridge top walk is a pleasure for the confident. In windy weather, and for anyone unsure of tackling the ascent/ridge/descent, we have a low level short walk option suitable for all.

Access by car: Park on the road past the massive **Hotel Beatriz** before the road swings left.

Access by bus: N°1 **Arrecife** to **Costa Teguise** and N°3 **Puerto del Carmen** via **Arrecife** to **Costa Teguise**. From the most easterly bus stop (near **Hotel Salinas** on **Avenida Islas Canarias**, off **Avenida del Mar**) take pavements approximately NW to the **Hotel Beatriz**.

> **Short Walk**
> Follow main route to the trail crossroads at Wp.4, then turn right to follow the lower trail as it contours around the *caldera* to the trail crossroads at Wp.8; then resume the main route.

Starting out on the western pavement (Wp.1 0M), we walk away from the resort, a ruin ahead of us on a small spur as the road and pavement swing left to climb past a pretty valley on our right, contrasting with the harsh *malpaís* elsewhere. The spiny aulaga or Lanzarote firebush (Launaea arborescens) and saltbush (Suaeda vermiculata) invade the pavement, slowly returning this failed urbanisation back to nature, as we swing right to walk through the largely barren *malpaís* in a gentle ascent. Our pavement climbs up to a crest, and as it curves left we step off onto a jeep track (Wp.2 14M).

The track runs across open ground toward a gap in a stone wall. Passing a small trail off to our right (Wp.3), we climb up to the gap to find two large stone cairns which mark the trail to the base of **Montaña Corona**. It is easy walking along the trail to pass a large cairn and stone designs, better seen from the peak, to arrive at a crossroads of trails (Wp.4 24M).

Montaña Corona stands out clearly ahead

For our Short Walk, turn right here and follow the trail round the *caldera* to the large stone cairn on a spur (Wp.8).

Montaña Corona looks both big and steep from this viewpoint, so girding our loins we set off up the lower slope on the stony trail, easier as an ascent than descent. The trail zigzags, more for artistic reasons than for any practical use, as we take frequent stops on this 'puff and grunt' climb. Our path disappears as we come onto bedrock, those stone designs by the crossroads much clearer from this elevated position. Our ascent is not vertiginous in the normal sense, but is developing into a steep almost scrambling climb; face the slope not the views when taking a break. We come slowly up past small volcanic blowholes, heading for the highest point above us, until finally we come up onto the summit of **Montaña Corona** (Wp.5 50M).

After that slightly unnerving climb, we gratefully take in the extensive views. Although we are only at 232 metres altitude, the low plains give the impression of a much higher altitude. Thoughtfully the rocks on the summit make for comfortable seating allowing us to enjoy a break before tackling the descent.

From the high point our return route is along the rock ridge of the *caldera*, a far more comfortable open ground route than our earlier ascent. We set off, (Wp.5 0M) picking our way carefully over the rocks and edge round a large boulder; this is definitely a 'Stop, and look at the view' section of the route.

... Montaña de Saga is a beautiful cone of reds and browns ...

Montaña de Saga is a beautiful cone of reds and browns to the north of us as we cross a broad rock cap to the ridge (Wp.6) before negotiating a trench through the ridge by caves. We are now curving south and descending through rough terrain to the second height point (Wp.7 12M).

A grit/shale path leads straight down the slope towards the large stone cairn on the saddle below, the path zigzagging as it loses height but this is still a very picky, slippery descent before arriving at the crossroads of trails (Wp.8 78M) just above the big stone cairn; our short walk option arriving here from the west.

Most walkers now plunge past the cairn and down the slippery, picky, loose shale trail to the flood plain fifty metres below, but if like us you have had enough of uncomfortable descents then we have a slightly longer but much more civilised alternative. From the crossroads we go left (N) on a narrow trail which curves round the mountain to a faint path junction (Wp.9 81M) where we keep right to descend amongst the foothills as our trail curves towards the resort. A faint trail goes onto a low rise as we continue down the small valley to cross its water runoff, where our trail is reduced to a trace crossing the flood plain towards a small cairn of stones (Wp.10 89M) where we meet the main path.

There are traces of paths almost everywhere on the flood plain, and the low ridges and big mountain offer no navigational sighting points; just the sort of country where GPS waypoint navigation scores highly. From the cairn we follow the sandy trail (SSW) to a junction where we go right and then a path joins us from the left, shortly followed by a path off to our right. We keep straight on the main path to close with old stone walls lining the valley, where we start climbing gently up past terraces abandoned millennia ago; do not pay any attention to white painted supposed cairns, as these are land boundary markers. We take a faint path going up by a wall to climb up onto a low ridge (Wp.11 99M) where **Costa Teguise** comes into view.

Ahead a path runs across to the wall (Wp.3 on our outward route) while we go left on a fainter trail to meet a stone wall (Wp.12) where we swing right (S) to head towards the **Hotel Beatriz**. Our trail heads down beside a stone wall, getting stonier underfoot as we head for the ruin seen at the start of our walk. We come down to a corner of the stone walled field (sic) to take a path which comes down onto a clearer trail which follows a small stony valley. Our path widens to a track passing a path on our left as the valley flattens out and our car comes into view ahead and we curve away from the water runoff to come back onto the pavement beside our start point (112M) at the end of our compact adventure.

We like coastal walks, whether they be on promenades for easy strolling or out along wild coastlines such as 'Peña del Rubicón' and 'A Path Between Two Seas'. Here we follow the coastal paths and tracks from **Arrieta** via **Charco del Palo** and **Los Cocoteros** to the outskirts of **Costa Teguise**. On the maps it looks like a flat stroll, but there are more than enough sharp ups and downs in the second part of the route, which combined with the distance, easily justify a 4 walker rating. This pristine, wild coastline is exposed to the elements so cover up against the sun and take plenty of drinking water.

Charco del Palo has good swimming in natural pools protected from the waves. It was the first official naturist resort established in the Canaries; as a hiker you might feel a bit overdressed there.

Los Cocoteros is largely holiday homes, meaning it's quiet in the week but can be busy at weekends and fiestas when their owners take a break from city life in Arrecife to decamp to the coast. It's way off the tourist track and as the locals usually bring their supplies with them, there are no tourist facilities such as cafés and bars as in **Charco del Palo**.

Access by car:
Long linear route not really suited to car drivers, but if you do rely on a car and want to do this route you can park in **Costa Teguise** and bus to **Arrieta** with a bus change in **Tahíche**.

Access by bus:
To get to the start, take line 7 or 9. Alight in **Arrieta** at a T-junction next to a supermarket. Neither **Charco del Palo** nor **Los Cocoteros** are served by bus.

We start from a T-junction at a bus stop and supermarket (Wp.1 0M) following

Our start at Wp.1

the street (sign 'Playa La Garita beach 500mts') SW and keeping straight on at all junctions until the end of the street where steps take us down to the beach (Wp.2 5M). Along the beach, we pass a *chiringuito* bar, then **Bar/Rest Casa de la Playa**, after which we follow the dirt track to pass a humble football ground and walk between dunes and old terraces to a Y-junction of tracks (Wp.3 18M).

Bearing left, we go almost to the end of the beach where a path climbs to the right to a ruined fort-like wall of a house before which it swings left for us to reach a plateau. We head towards a compound walled in stones and várious clutter. Our path turns slightly inland to bypass the private property, crossing a pair of its access tracks forming a skew crossroads (Wp.4 25M), before

LC returning to the coast.

We head towards two houses, crossing a bare rock gully level with the first house, then keep left at a Y-junction to pass an old swimming pool (Wp.5 39M) below the second house.

Our path joins a sandy track below outcrops of lava, at the end of which we keep left to find a clear sandy path. Ignoring a right-hand dirt track heading inland, we maintain our distance from the coast to cross a rock gully (Wp.6 48M), after which our path levels off and undulates across the badlands as views open up ahead of us. We descend into a bowl where we join the end of a dirt track, which crosses a broad watercourse before coming to a junction at an old pool (Wp.7 57M) where the left-hand track doubles back to a protected sea-water pool, **Piscina natural Robayna**.

Maintaining direction, we are now on a broad well-driven dirt road, which runs through ruined walls after which it swings right. In this bend, we branch off on the second of the two left-hand dirt tracks (Wp.8 60M), immediately passing a huge stone spiral. We get sand underfoot as we

Huge stone spiral (Wp.8)

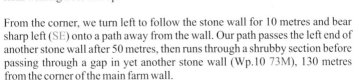

climb gently, bearing straight ahead at a double crossroads to pass to the left of a house. It is gently up and down around sand dunes as the surface changes to a fine *picón*, before coming to a T-junction (Wp.9 69M), where the left branch immediately crosses a watercourse, while we bear right (W, then briefly SW) to come to the corner of a dry-stone wall of a farm with fig trees and opuntia.

From the corner, we turn left to follow the stone wall for 10 metres and bear sharp left (SE) onto a path away from the wall. Our path passes the left end of another stone wall after 50 metres, then runs through a shrubby section before passing through a gap in yet another stone wall (Wp.10 73M), 130 metres from the corner of the main farm wall.

Maintaining direction (SE), a path joins us from the right, before we briefly join a sandy track coming from the left. After 30 metres, at a Y-junction (Wp.11 76M), we turn left onto a path which soon takes us from the Sahara-like land onto a rough *malpaís*, where we skirt a stone wall on our right before leaving it to pass a cluster of *tabaibas* and come to pass through stone walls (Wp.12 81M); here we join a dirt track running south (S). Our track is lined by ruined walls before it runs through an S-bend amongst lava outcrops to widen again. After the S-bend, our track runs in an uninterrupted straight line for 1.2 kilometres.

A pool in Charco del Palo

We keep straight ahead at all junctions, passing a neat house on our right (Wp.13 93M). A gentle climb brings us onto a tarmac street in **Charco del Palo**.

Bearing left into the second left-hand street, **Calle Punta del Pasito** (Wp.14 104M), we follow it to its end, where we take the steps (Wp.15 108M) down to the main *charco* protected from ocean waves, with well-made sandy terraces ideal for sun-bathing. We follow the coastal path, passing in front of **Charco Natural** bungalows (Wp.16 116M); a path off to our right across the open space leads to a near-by supermarket, Centro Comercial and restaurants; the only opportunity for refreshments along this route.

Refreshed (0M), we keep following the coast, passing a second natural swimming pool before the last apartments opposite a nice circle of stones (Wp.17 4M) and leave the settlement. Our coastal trail becomes a dirt track before reverting to a trail (Wp.18 12M). We ignore minor inland branches to pass through remains of a stone wall, then bear right at a Y-junction, our cairn-marked branch passing a little memorial cross off to our left. Past the end of a stone wall (Wp.19 19M), we follow the rugged coast to squeeze between sturdy *corrals*, after

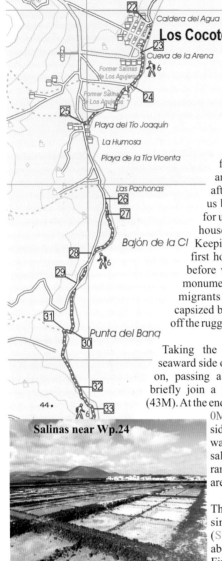

Caldera del Agua

Los Cocoteros

Cueva de la Arena

Former Salinas de Los Agujeros

Former Salina de Los Agujeros

Playa del Tío Joaquín

La Humosa

Playa de la Tía Vicenta

Las Pachonas

Bajón de la Cl

Punta del Banq

Salinas near Wp.24

44.

which we climb in deeper sand along a path lined by stones.

We come to a group of windbreaks (Wp.20 24M) before a short steep clamber brings us onto a wall of lava to pass round the edge of a wild bay. We come into view of houses and **Los Cocoteros** further ahead as we pass a rock arch at a collapsed sea cave, after which yellow arrows guide us between walls to pass houses for us to emerge on a dirt track at a house entrance (Wp.21 29M). Keeping straight on, we come the first houses of **Los Cocoteros**, just before which there is a small pillar monument (Wp.22 37M) to 25 African migrants who died here in their capsized boat literally just a few metres off the rugged coast in 2009.

Taking the concrete walkway on the seaward side of the houses we keep straight on, passing a playground, until we very briefly join a pavement of the main road (43M). At the end of the chrome railing (Wp.23 0M) we walk round the seaward side of the houses to take a well-walked trail heading towards the salt pans where we find a boat ramp (Wp.24 7M) and parking area.

There's a myriad of trails so we simply choose one heading (SW) towards houses built above **Playa del Tío Joaquin**. First, we pass a fort-like hut at the edge of old salt pans before joining a dirt track, leaving it as it sweeps inland, as we follow a walking trail along the foreshore. Across a gully, our trail climbs steeply up onto the headland, inland of the houses to come onto a broad dirt road (Wp.25 20M).

Now it's an easy stroll down the dirt road, leaving the houses behind as we pass the big pebble beach of **Playa de la Tía Vicenta** and two minor tracks off right before coming to a fork (Wp.26 33M) where we take the minor rough track to our front left. This track soon reduces to a walking trail as we start climbing onto the headland before dropping down to a sandy area with *zoco* wind shelters (Wp.27 36M).

Our onward trail takes us along the coastline to drop down into a shallow valley and then climbing up to the top of the cliffs to join a dirt track (Wp.28 46M), the same dirt track we left at Wp.26. After eighty metres on the track, we leave it again as it swings right while we continue on a narrow, cairn-marked trail above lava slopes that run down to the sea. We come back to the track again for a few metres before it takes us down into a shallow valley marked by a large *zoco* wind shelter (Wp.29 53M).

Our climb out of the valley brings us onto a headland where our trail becomes fainter; we are guided (S) by cairns to come above the mouth of a small barranco (Wp.30 60M). Taking what might loosely be described as a trail, we descend along the northern side of the cleft by picking a line of least resistance through the boulders to come down onto the barranco's pebble beach, just inland of which is a small lagoon. Facing south-west, we clamber up through the rocks to find ourselves on a walking trail (Wp.31 64M) that has taken a long inland loop to cross the barranco.

Keeping to the cliff-top trail, we ignore branches towards the sea as we walk through an area of sea-spray covered cliffs before coming down into a lava-block valley (Wp.32 76M). Now a steady ascent brings us up around the head of the cliffs, to the view of yet more cliffs ahead. It is a picky descent down to a sandy valley floor (Wp.33 81M) followed by another steady climb up to the top of the cliffs again.

Now we are rewarded for our efforts by possibly the best views on the whole route (Wp.34 83M). For once, we can now make steady progress along the cliffs (SE & S) without too many sharp inclines as we pass above a sharp inlet in the cliffs (Wp.35 93M).

As we get closer to **Costa Teguise** and the settlement of **Ancones** we start to see a plethora of possible trails. In these potentially confusing conditions, our rule is to take the main trail heading (S to SW) towards the resort; most of the trail splits rejoin again shortly after the split.

A hundred metres after a cairned trail leads off towards the 52 metre peak our trail has a major split (Wp.36 106M) where we take the inland right hand option; you could take the seaward left hand option but it involves more ups and downs before rejoining three hundred metres later (Wp.37 111M). The desert settlement of **Ancones** is away on our right, while our trail takes us down into a valley littered with lava blocks directly below the settlement's houses where we come onto a track running up the valley to **Ancones**.

At a junction we take a walking trail left to another track that leads to one of the surprises of this route. We've been walking through wild untamed landscapes, of which this valley is typical so it is a surprise to happen upon a neatly built lava block wall that edges wide lava laid steps heading down to the sea (Wp.38 116M). At the next path junction we take the inland option and go straight over the next path crossroads which brings us to a steep, picky descent to a parking area next to the sea (Wp.39 120M).

We take the walking trail's continuation from the parking area, another option is to take the dirt track accessing the parking area, ignoring a minor path a little later as we head (S) directly towards the resort and come onto the dirt track (Wp.40 130M) that serves **Ancones**. Now it is simply striding out along the broad dirt road until we come onto the end of the promenade (Wp.41 148M). Along the promenade we pass the **Sands Beach Resort** and then cut across a large car park (Wp.42 152M) to the **Avenida de las Islas Canarias** (Wp.43 155M) a few metres east of a taxi rank.

While this is our official finish, where you stop depends upon your plans. For refreshments, you could stay on the promenade to indulge in the Brit and Irish bars facing **Playa Cucharas**, though our choice would be to continue west on **Avenida de las Islas Canarias** to the choice of cafés behind **Centro Comercial Las Cucharas** or **Helga's Cafe** off the western end of the car parking.

view from Montaña Blanca's summit

Not to be confused with the spectacular **Caldera Blanca** bordering the **Timanfaya** national park, **Montaña Blanca** between **Tías** and **San Bartolomé**, at 599 metres is one of the highest volcanoes of the island and along with its more famous namesake it is another absolute stunner. Seen from the LZ-2 road, it looks majestic with its southern flanks cracked by a myriad of gullies, making it look inpenetrable. The view from the north discloses lush green pastures and old stone walls set high up its slopes. The rim of the grassy caldera, nestling higher than most of the craters in Lanzarote, is already a great vantage point, but the views get even better if we climb along the rim to the summit trig point, from where we overlook a substantial part of Lanzarote!

If that's not enough, the southern slopes are an archaeological site with ancient carvings and also conceal a unique water deposit system; *maretas*, huge underground tanks over 50 metres in length that were constructed to collect water off **Montaña Blanca's** slopes.

* at the bar adjacent to the church, or further down in the village

Access by car: From the intersection of LZ-35 and LZ-301, take the LZ-301 for 680 metres (WNW) before turning left into **Montaña Blanca** village. Follow **Calle Lomo de Tesa** all the way to the church where there is plenty of parking.

Access by bus: Take line 32 (**Arrecife/Playa Honda**) and alight in **Montaña Blanca** at the **Colegio** bus stop. Walk up the street (W) for 100 metres to reach the church.

Short versions:
a) Omit the summit. At the stone hut (Wp.12) take the descending path (NW) to Wp.16 (5.5km, Ascents and descents 320m).
b) From Wp.3, take the path down to the pallet hut and climb directly (SE) to the crater (Wp.12) via our return route and then make the summit circuit (4km, Ascents and descents 300m).

Our start is at **Maria Auxiliadora** church (Wp.1 0M) to briefly follow **Calle Lomo de Tesa** (W), then **Calle La Degollada** (SW) to climb gently along the tarmac lane. At house No.6 (Wp.2 5M) we continue on a broad dirt track,

Wp1
Maria Auxiliadora church

passing **Finca Tierrita Machares** on our right. We note a parallel dirt track running below us on our left (**GR131**), from which we'll have two links back on our main track later on the return: either a track we pass just after the last corrals, or a path a bit later (Wp.3 10M) coming from a strange pallet hut. Staying on our upper track we spot a trail down from the mountain feeding onto the lower parallel track just after the pallet hut - that's our return route from the crater.

Our track is joined by the **GR131** before reaching its highest point at a saddle (Wp.4 16M), bringing the coast and Fuerteventura into view. Old stone walls dominate the slopes on either side of the pass, where a faint track forks off to the right. Keeping straight on, we stroll down the dirt track, enjoying far views, before crossing a concreted watercourse where we are joined by another track from the right. Passing a house with a tall fence where a *pista* goes off to the left, leading to a very noisy dog 'shelter', we leave the fenced plot on our left, our track running between meadows before passing a faint track that forks off to the right just after which we join a large *picón* field on the left.

At the end of this large field (Wp.5 29M) we come to a junction, where we leave the **GR131** and turn left to follow a faint jeep track steeply up, skirting the *picón* field until its upper edge, where we turn right (SE). Walking across open ground for 50 metres, we find a track splitting into two branches (Wp.6

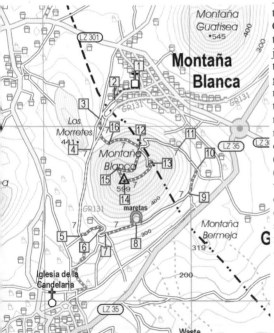

33M) as it runs down the mountain. Crossing the split track, we turn east to join a cairn-marked track, which crosses a gully just above a ravine. When our track turns downhill (30 metres after the ravine), we turn left onto a clear path (Wp.7 36M), heading (E, then NNE) to an SL waypost, where we come onto a cream-coloured rough surface to reach a large notice board; the most difficult navigation of the route is now over.

We traverse the southern slopes of the mountain along the rock path climbing gently in the broken land strewn with gullies to squeeze through a shoulder-high carved rock to come onto a dirt track with two water tanks (Wp.8 42M) built inside the mountain and a notice board explaining the *maretas*.

Now it's easy downhill along the access track for the *maretas*. Our *pista* becomes badly eroded before swinging right through a sharp dogleg bend (Wp.9 51M), at which point we leave it to continue straight across open ground (NE, then NNE). This pathless section of 350 metres is straight forward; all we have to do is to maintain height as we traverse the slope. Luckily, the eroded badlands of the southern flanks affect only the higher slopes making for easy progress as we circle the mountain. We cross some minor gullies to come to a view of **Montaña Guatisea's** white cone, which becomes our bearing, before joining a dirt track (Wp.10 57M), 100 metres north-west of a farmstead.

Our dirt track climbs steadily to steeply (NW) away from the farm, passing impressive gullies before we bear left just before a fenced reservoir (Wp.11 63M). We climb in tight zigzags to pass above a transmitter, after which the gradient briefly eases before reverting to a steep climb, relieved by great views. Two more switchbacks bring us to a stone hut (Wp.12 77M) at the northern rim of the shallow grassy *caldera*, **Hoya de la Cruz**, its edge defined by an old stone wall.

Noting the cross set on the ridge 200 metres to the south-east, we continue climbing along the dirt track which skirts the eastern edge of the crater. 30 metres before the end of the track, we bear left on a faint path, which doubles back traversing the slope to join the ridge, where we turn north to climb across the rocky terrain to the wooden cross (Wp.13 83M). Following the rim further up, we pass a pair of windbreaks before reaching the trig point and antenna at

wooden cross at Wp.13

the summit of **Montaña Blanca** (Wp.14 91M). One of Lanzarote's best vantage points allows us to overlook more than half of the island!

From the peak (0M), we descend (NW) along the rim for 160 metres until our path swings sharp right (Wp.15 3M) to take us down to the caldera floor over a short section of deep *picón*. Crossing the caldera floor, we come back to the hut (Wp.12 10M), where we cross the stone wall to its northern side.

From below the hut, a clear path descends (NW) down the green slopes, the path becoming stone-littered after running through short zigzags. It then becomes covered in *picón* (Wp.16 17M) and joins an old stone wall as we come down to the pallet hut (20M), 70 metres south of Wp.3. To get onto the higher parallel track, we cut across via the path or further down along the connecting *pista*, before returning back to the church (31M).

197 metres might not sound like much of a mountain, but located where it is in the flat deserts of **Playa Blanca**, this counts as a high summit. Easy wayfinding on well marked paths with enough of a climb for a sense of achievement, this is a popular ascent, perhaps because it is such a contrast to the featureless resort development. A route for all ages; we were accompanied by a three year old boy and his parents on our latest visit.

Short Walk option - this *is* the short walk.

Access by bus:
N°60 from **Arrecife** to **Playa Blanca** bus station, from where there are two choices. Either walk inland (N) along the main road to pass the petrol station and go left (W) at the roundabout, strolling along the **Avenida Faro Pechiguera** pavement to the second roundabout where we go right on **Calle Francia** (N) to come gently uphill to **Paradise Island Club**, where we turn left (W) onto **Avenida Noruega** to our official start at Wp.1. Adds 2½ km to the route.

Alternatively, take the N°30 **Playa Blanca** town bus from the town's bus station (a rather roundabout route) to **Virginia Park** which is 2 stops after the school (*Colegio*). Walk south towards the sea for a few metres, then first right is **Avenida Noruega.**

Access by car:
If you are driving, we suggest parking at the outer fringes of the development.

At last we are heading for the mountain, passing **Los Claveles** on our left as we head uphill to the road junction alongside **Montaña Baja** development; drivers should park on the road in this general area.

A giant pebble points the way

The 'Al Volcan' sign (Wp.1 0M) points us up the road, to a street junction (Wp.2). Development scourge has meant that the old start to the path has been cut off by an abandoned development so we walk up the street to the end of the fence where the path now starts.

It's a dusty sloping path that winds its way up towards the ridge, passing a path coming from the left (Wp.3, and an alternative start route) and bringing us onto the broad back of the ridge (Wp.4 15M) to meet a dirt road coming in from the north.

Our ascent of Montaña Roja lies ahead

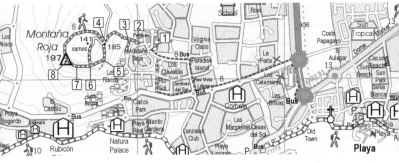

Our choice is to go left to circle the crater clockwise, gently uphill overlooking a large array of 'stone names' which have been laid out on the floor of the *caldera*.

Stone names decorate the floor of the *caldera*

Following our ascent, we now have an easy stroll with views over the new hotels to **Papagayo beach**. At a path junction (Wp.5) we have an optional peak to visit on our left, or can go down to a saddle (Wp.6) where a path descends into the *caldera*, an optional steep short cut. Continuing round the crater rim, we have a climbing section alongside lichen-covered rocks to a saddle viewpoint (Wp.7) and then a moderately serious ascent up to the trig point (Wp.8 27M).

After the trig point we pass another saddle viewpoint, after which our trail descends, curving right and flattening out for an easy stroll along to the dirt track into the *caldera*. Now it is gently up to meet our upward path (Wp.4 40M) on the wide ridge, and back down the dusty trail to our car - or if using the bus, a longer stroll back into the resort or to await the town bus N°30 back to the bus station.

Playa de Papagayo is Lanzarote's most famous beach. It is easy to reach by car from the roundabout on the **Playa Blanca - Femés** road on the signed tracks after paying your entrance fee; note that your hire-car insurance does not cover you for off-tarmac driving. From the large parking area behind the cliff top bars we simply follow the paths for the steep descent to, and ascent from, this cliff-enclosed perfect beach.

We feel that the beauty of **Papagayo** is enhanced by expending a bit of effort in gaining the reward. **Playas Mujeres** and **Pozo**, which we cross on the way to **Papagayo**, are also beautiful cozzie-optional beaches. So to make a day of it, take your cozzie - or not, as the mood takes you - and enjoy the best beaches on the island, their beauty enhanced by the barren surroundings in which they are found.

Access by bus:

30 service from **Playa Blanca** bus station to its eastern end at **Las Coloradas** then follow the blue signs onto **Calle de las Buganvillas** and down to our start.

Access by car:

From the roundabout at the edge of the old town we go left (there is no other way) to head east on **Avenida Papagayo**, keeping on the main road until we see the blue (walker) **Playa de Papagayo** signs; yellow signs direct cars onto the dirt road and 'gate fee' route for drivers. We follow the blue signs until we see the final sign directing walkers onto a cinder track. Now we look for an on-street parking place on the road up to the **Papagayo Arena Hotel**.

We follow the blue sign (Wp.1 0M) up the cinder track to pass between the boulders barring vehicle access and climb up to a junction (Wp.2) behind the hotel. Taking a faint track to the left to come up onto the desert plateau - featureless except for the trig point on our front left.

Signs point the way at Wp.1

Keeping to the faint track we come up a rise that brings the beaches into view as our route curves right past a cairn to a faint junction (Wp.3) where we keep straight on towards the distant car park. Strolling over the headland we are joined by trails from our right as we come to the top of a steep trail (Wp.4) which gives us a skittery descent down to the back of **Playa Mujeres** (Wp.5 16M) beside the first car park.

Walking across the rear of the beach behind the dunes, we pass the second car park (Wp.6) to a choice of a steep sandy path which runs up from the beach, or we can continue ahead up a sandy *barranco*, followed by an open-ground

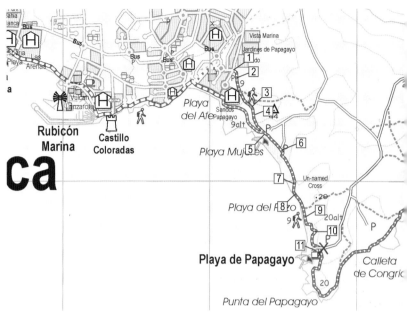

ascent over rock onto the next headland - our choice.

Cairns provide approximate direction markers to the start of a path (Wp.7) dropping down to **Playa del Pozo**, the path finishing in a small rock scramble to drop us onto the beach (Wp.8 30M). Straight across the beach, we head for a path (Wp.9) climbing the sloping rock face onto the next headland.

We climb up the path, the sand changing to purple rock as we come onto the headland, the car park now much closer as we cross a water-eroded gully (Wp.10) followed by an ascent, and crossing a second gully before coming up to the bars above **Papagayo beach** (Wp.11 45M).

Past the bar's generator, a manicured walkway is signed to the beach taking us between the bars. There's a choice of three bars for refreshments and, given their spectacularly isolated position, prices are very reasonable; regard a refreshment stop on their terrace as compulsory, and enjoy the views down onto Lanzarote's best beach.

Papagayo beach

If you are planning on sunbathing, take one of the steep paths which lead down to the perfect beach, though take care on their slippery surfaces, and it will be (of course) an equally steep climb back up.

Deserts have a strange unreality all of their own. Driving across the **Rubicón** desert, there's a sense that nothing has happened here in aeons; walking there gives an even greater sense of timelessness - it's easy to imagine that whole civilisations might have disappeared under the wastes of the world's great deserts. Our excursion is along the seaward margin of the **Rubicón**, passing some beautiful rock pools set in the lava foreshore, to the *peña* of this desert, the long-abandoned **Atlante del Sol Hotel**, a monument to the foolishness of investing in the desert.

Our short option is an 'Out & Back' to the **Atlante del Sol**, while our full route is an adventurous but easy route skirting the dramatic lava cliff coast between the wild Atlantic (on our left) and the **Rubicón** desert (on our right), it has a wilderness feel all the way until we overlook **Las Salinas**. Sun protection and plenty of drinking water are essential.

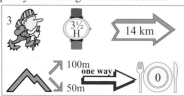

Access by bus:
From **Playa Blanca** bus station the 30 service runs as far as **Faro Park** from where we can walk through to join our route at Wp.4. If we walk it is a 5.5km stroll along the western coastal promenade to our start at the *faro*. Bus back from **La Hoya** bus stop on the 60.

Access by car: 2CSK Route
Park one car at the *faro*, and the second car at the parking area at Wp.20.

Faro de Pechiguera is actually twin light houses, one small and squat and one tall and imperíous (Wp.1 0M). From the lighthouses we leave on a small path beside a low wall which widens to a track which brings us up to a turning circle by the **Finistere** development (Wp.2 5M). Now we have the luxury of a promenade, but it doesn't last long and we are back on dirt track and trail until we climb over a boulder mound to come onto another turning circle (Wp.3 8M). Now we're back on a better financed promenade, strolling beside the foaming foreshore as we come along to the access into **Faro Park** development (Wp.4 16M).

Shortly, in 190 metres, the promenade finishes along with the houses, and we have a scruffy little section before coming onto a track, then taking a minor track ahead when the main track swings right, to cross a water runoff and come to a junction (Wp.5 28M) where a track goes right to the tarmac access road. Continuing ahead, we pass an isolated house on its seaward side, the track ending for us to negotiate the end of the property's wall and a runoff before coming onto a trail paralleling the coast. Our trail widens to a track and views open up over the nothingness of the **Rubicón** desert as we head for another isolated house.

As we close with the house **Atlante del Sol** comes into view. Approaching the house (Wp.6 38M), we find a street name 'Cala Malva 1'; the house is obviously owned by an optimist still awaiting the arrival of **Playa Blanca**'s outskirts.

As is the way of deserts, it's a surprise to find ugliness or nothingness, standing alongside something of great beauty - think of those **Papagayo** beaches backed by featureless, barren desert. It's the case here as, opposite the house, metal steps lead down the cliffs to a exciting lava foreshore containing beautiful rock pools. From the house we continue along the track running above the cliffs, a branch going out onto a 'table' headland (Wp.7), the track becoming sandy as we pass a small lava peak (Wp.8). Our track goes left in front of a lava wall while we go left on a trace of a track which soon peters out among the lava-topped cliffs. Ahead, our destination of **Atlante del Sol** seems close as we come inland to seek a route amongst the tracery of faint tracks and trails which dissect the rock-littered sandy desert. We weave our way across the plain, passing a walled farm on our right to come upon the unexpected sight of a swampy lagoon in front of the fire-darkened shell of the hotel. Skirting the noisome waters, we pass on the seaward side of the first wing and walk across the open ground to the far wing (Wp.9 66M).

Standing by this financial and physical ruin that once was someone's expected boom town, the power of the desert and the ability of its nothingness to absorb even the best laid plans and investments is palpable.

Of course there are now far bigger monuments to developers' greed littering the southern edge of the desert, but it's a chilling thought that **Atlante del Sol** has stood abandoned for over three decades. Our Shorter Option is to return from here to the *faro*, but today we're off across the desert heading for **Las Salinas** and the **La Hoya** bus stop to catch a ride back to **Playa Blanca**.

From the hotel's northern corner (0M) we walk out over the open ground (approx. E) to come onto a faint track, just slightly more cleared than the surrounding desert, which curves away from the sea (E) and gradually becomes more track-like as we come onto a well-used track (Wp.10 8M). That's the difficult navigation over as we turn left to follow the rough track (don't even think of bringing your hire car here) as it heads towards the coastline (NE). It's easy strolling along the undulating track which flattens as we progress, and splits for a short section before passing a *zoco* style wind shelter (Wp.11 21M); deserts have lots of natural features but anything man-made is a rarity, even a dry stone wind shelter.

With Atlantic rollers crashing into the lava cliffs on our left, this section can seem like strolling through sea mist accompanied by whale-like noises created by hidden blow holes, until we pass a second *zoco* style shelter

(Wp.12 27M), our track now taking a northerly aspect towards the **Punta de Piedra Alta**, rather a grand name for a trig point set on top of the cliffs.

Just after our track divides (Wp.13 35M), you might like to walk over to the cliffs to see rock-climbing fittings that allow cliff mountaineers to abseil down to the lava-shelf foreshore by the **El Convento** cave; most impressive if you happen to see them in use. Black cubist rocks decorate the cliff top plateau on the section before we come opposite the trig point (Wp.14 42M) to walk across the open ground and from beside the trig point (Wp.15) we have a superb view of lava shelf foreshore and sea-delved cave with the Atlantic rollers crashing over the shelf in a foaming mass, one of the most spectacular sea views on the island. Back on our track, we head for the desalination plant directly ahead. After a particularly rough section the track smooths out for us to make easy progress. As we close on the plant the track divides, the right hand track is clearer but both sections will lead us up to the parking area from where we walk up to the northern face of the plant (Wp.16 74M).

Atlante del Sol to the desalination plant (5km) has been easy walking, but looking north towards **Las Salinas**, we now face a broken landscape as the desert runs out. Despite first appearances, it is an easy section only requiring more concentration on where we're putting our feet as we stroll across (NE) to a track junction (Wp.17) where we keep ahead (NE) on a degraded rough rock track overlooking a small disused quarry; if you take the left fork at Wp.17 you'll be walking across the floor of the quarry to its wall of tumbled rocks where a cairn marked path climbs up to join our main route (Wp.18).

We stay on the rough track; in 120 metres a path goes down to our front left. We can either stay on the higher rough track or take the lower trail, both options rejoining 280 metres later (Wp.19) after the high route has come

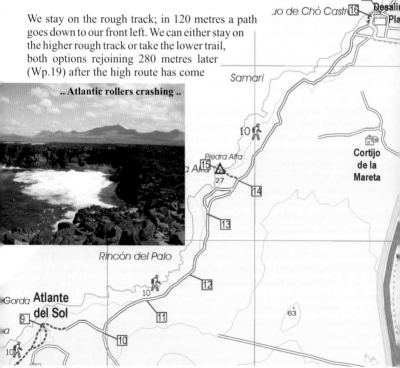

.. Atlantic rollers crashing ..

onto a better track which runs out at this point.

Ahead of us (NE) is the welcome sight of a walking trail snaking up and down, in and out, of the tumbled landscape. After all that walking on desert tracks it's very satisfying to be on a trail that's the only choice of route. We wind our way towards the small car park above the **Las Salinas** sand bar. As we close with the car park there are higher and lower options which come together again as we step off the trail at the bottom of the dirt road access from the LZ-701 (Wp.20 97M).

On the narrow trail towards Las Salinas

Below us, trails lead down onto the sand bar that protects the **Las Salinas** salt pans from the fury of the Atlantic, and across the bar to another car park on the far side. The bar runs down to an exciting beach but on no account should you be tempted to swim here as the currents can be treacherous. Across the salt pans is the inviting sight of a bar/restaurant that isn't on our route but you could be tempted into a diversion if the bus timetable allows. See our Walk 11 'Salinas de Janubio' route to extend this walk, taking in the colourful salt pans.

It's been an interesting route so far and it would be good to say that the excitement lasts right up to the end but sadly, we're now into the boring piece of getting to the bus stop. You could try cutting across the hills up to the road but more straightforward is an uphill slog to the LZ-701 road (Wp.21 105M), then turn north to walk along the road to the roundabout – be careful as although this is a quiet road, what traffic there is whizzes along as though its trying to outpace vehicles on the LZ-2 main road. Across the roundabout, it's just 180 metres to the **La Hoya** bus stop and shelter (Wp.22 123M). If your timing and the bus schedule allows it is an easy stroll down from the roundabout to the bar/restaurant picturesquely situated overlooking the salt pans but allow a good fifteen minutes uphill return in time to catch your bus back to **Playa Blanca**.

11 Salinas de Janubio

This very enjoyable and colourful stroll in a unique, impressive landscape is suited not just for birdwatchers, who are likely to find different species hanging around **Laguna de Janubio**, but for everyone in the mood for a less challenging, leisurely day out. In our short circular route tucked between two masses of water, we head out to follow shores of the tamed one, an emerald-green lagoon lined by the radiant salt pans, before returning alongside the wild ocean. The salt pans are the biggest in the Canaries, though only partly in operation now.

After the hike we recommend calling at **Mirador de Las Salinas** (Km2.3 of the LZ-703) overlooking the rectangular 'art' of the salt pans. The restaurant there is popular with locals and has a great terrace to enjoy the *salinas* from an elevated perspective while protected from the ever-present wind and sun.

| 1 | 40 M | 2½ km | 30m / 30m | ↻ | 4* |

*Mirador de Las Salinas

Access by car: take the LZ-703 skirting the northern flank of **Laguna de Janubio** and park at the gravel car park at Km3.7.

Access by bus: no bus connection.

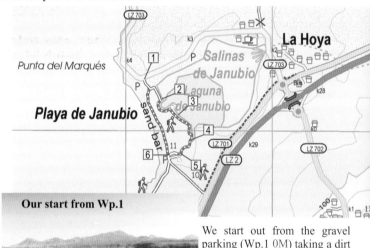

Our start from Wp.1

We start out from the gravel parking (Wp.1 0M) taking a dirt track descending to a junction of tracks at the first of the old salt pans, where we take the left-hand *pista* across blocks of lava. At a T-junction 30 metres later the track ahead is chained off, restricted to the salt-pans workers. We turn right to follow a straight track alongside the pans before coming over a spill of basalt boulders to the lagoon shore (Wp.2 5M); the old mill ahead of us in the distance is our next objective.

Approaching the old mill Wp.3

Now we simply follow the shore of **Laguna de Janubio**, passing a small promontory before coming to the old mill (Wp.3 10M), originally used to pump the sea water into the lagoon. Behind it we pass another ruin and a sturdy stone wall, after which we join salt pans on our right as we keep skirting the shore.

Nearing the embankment and Wp.5

Our trail swings south to follow a small inlet, its opposite side dominated by steep slopes. Leaving the lagoon, whose level may differ based on the season and how much water is pumped in, we pass the southern-most end of the salt pools (Wp.4 17M) to come to an area of gullies, bowls and mini-lagoons. We join a clear trail which follows an embankment and head towards two ruined houses. At the lower ruin, we reach a junction of dirt tracks (Wp.5 21M), where we take the first right-hand branch that takes us to the beach (Wp.6 25M) below a small parking area.

We follow the beach back to our starting point.

To commemorate the devastating volcanic eruptions of 1730-1736, in which the **Yaiza** region suffered the worst depredations, the local government built an elevated walkway and gardens running around the base of **Montaña Cinta**. This makes for easy strolling combined with views over the town to the lava sea and **Timanfaya**.

Unfortunately, they forgot to complete the centre section of the walkway, thus requiring us to do a little traditional path walking to join the two sections. They also forgot to tell anyone that these gardens exist, so although tour buses park near our start, you are likely to have the **Volcanic Gardens** and their views to yourself.

Access by bus:
N°60 and N°161serve **Yaiza**.
Access by car:
Park off the old main road through **Yaiza** behind the church, where there is plenty of on-street parking and an official car park in front of the police station.

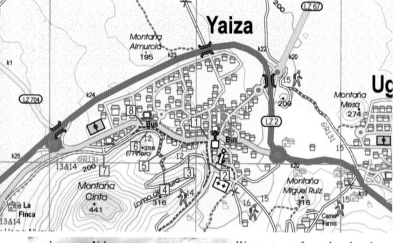

... views over Yaiza ...

We start out from the church (Wp.1 0M) to walk south past government administration buildings (note the 'Educación, Cultura y Festivos' office on the left, where you may be able to pick up their 'Ruta de Caballos' leaflet) to a multi-street junction with a confusion of traffic arrows painted on the roadway.

On our front right is a lava wall containing planted gardens and a wide rock stairway, which we climb to come onto a broad red cinder track (Wp.2). The most energetic section of the route is already completed, as we turn right to stroll along the elevated walkway taking in the views over **Yaiza** town.

Our stroll curves around the hillside to the end of the first section of gardens (Wp.3), the second section of gardens facing us across a valley as we continue on a dirt track along the southern side of the valley. The fields on the valley floor are edged with earth mounds, and at the the end of the second large field (Wp.4 10M) the track continues ahead while we go right onto a path which runs along the top of an earth mound (NW).

Views to Montaña Cinta from the path

Aloes along the route

At the northern side of the field we swing right, dropping down to cross a gully between the mounds, and then left (NW) along another mound to come up onto a disused track (Wp.5). Going right, we come down the track, which narrows to a trail after an earth mound to reach the red cinder track at the second section of the 'Volcanic Gardens'(17M).

With the cross-country section behind us, it is back to easy strolling as we curve round the mountain to come above the **El Campo Bar/Rest**, where an access stairway drops down to the road (Wp.6).

Both sections of the **Volcanic Gardens** have been well planted; the Aloe plants and Euphorbia varieties that line the track are particularly fine specimens, so it's a great disappointment when this planting runs out and the final section resembles a scene of crucifixion rather than a garden, with young saplings staked out to die without water on the barren slopes.

At the end of this depressing section a dirt track continues round the mountain to **La Finca**, while we go right (Wp.7 25M) down a steep track that drops us down to the access road for the outlying houses of **Yaiza**. Once on the access track, we head right towards the old main road and **El Campo**, passing some scruffy houses before reaching the main road where we choose to take a refreshment stop in **El Campo Bar/Rest** (Wp.8 30M). Our return is to simply walk along the pavement, up to our starting point at the church.

A big walk in Lanzarote's context, which follows the new **GR131** across vast plains, allows us to enjoy expansive views of the south. Once we get out of the not-too-inspiring streets of **Playa Blanca**, we are about to experience a wild vastness and solitude of sheer plains and *malpaís* on our way to **Las Breñas**, where we have a choice of great refreshments, before setting off for the second leg of the route to **Yaiza**, a section quite rich with splendid panoramic vistas. Check the weather forecast before planning this trip - in case of strong northern wind it is better to postpone this one - you don't want to end up battling against the wind as the route in its entirety follows a north-easterly course.

4 | 3¾ H | 14 km | 280m one way / 120m | 5

Access by car: Park in **Yaiza** at a car park 100 metres SW of Wp.24 next to the plaza and bus to the start in **Playa Blanca**; the bus stop in **Yaiza** is 200 metres E along **Calle Vista de Yaiza**. Or park in **Playa Blanca** behind the bus station, and return by bus from **Yaiza**.

Access by bus: The 60 runs between **Arrecife**, **Yaiza** and **Playa Blanca**, and the 161 between **Puerto del Carmen**, **Yaiza** and **Playa Blanca**.

Starting from **Playa Blanca** bus station (Wp.1 0M), we follow the pavement
Wp.3 start of trail   (NE) to the large roundabout, which we cross via a zebra

crossing to join **Avenida a Femés**. We follow the pavement (NE) along the road past another roundand then **Cay Beach Sun Hotel** (Wp.2 13M), before coming out of town. 30 metres after the 'Playa Blanca' sign, we find a GR signpost and a trail (Wp.3 22M) heading north.

Taking the boulder lined trail (N) we swing left before springing over rubble onto a dirt track (Wp.4 27M). We follow the track (N), skirting an abandoned compound and piles of rubble. Our surroundings improve as our track swings left to round the corner of the compound before turning right (N) 100 metres later, leaving the ghost town behind.

A track joins us from our left before we cross an eroded dirt road, 30 metres after which we bear right at a Y-junction (Wp.5 42M) onto a trail, passing under an electricity line. We are on a broad trail, which heads to a farmstead. Joining a stone wall of the farm and the dirt track that lines it, we bear left at a Y-junction at the corner of the wall. Small cairns guide us to cross the farm's access track (Wp.6 55M) to leave the very last homestead until **Las Breñas** behind, our track soon dwindling to a trail. Ignoring a broad stone-lined track to our right, we cross two ruined stone walls, after which our trail swings left. We round a large cairn on a rise before descending briefly, having views of **Las Breñas** far ahead of us.

Crossing a faint dirt track (Wp.7 67M), our trail levels off before we find ourselves climbing again. We circle a hillock before crossing two watercourses (Wp.8 77M). Hints of old terraces line our trail as the houses of **Las Breñas** get closer with each step. Passing a notice board on ancient settlements in the area, we join a stone wall (Wp.9 87M) on our right side. Traces of bygone farming are becoming more obvious as we have walls on both sides, before climbing to join a rough dirt track (Wp.10 94M). Bearing left, careful footwork is needed as our track is heavily eroded and rough, taking us up to join a dirt track at a signpost just before stepping onto the tarmac and the first house, **'Casa del Roble'**. Past the house we come to a road junction (Wp.11 103M) in **Las Breñas**.

Bearing right, we take **Calle los Roques** to walk

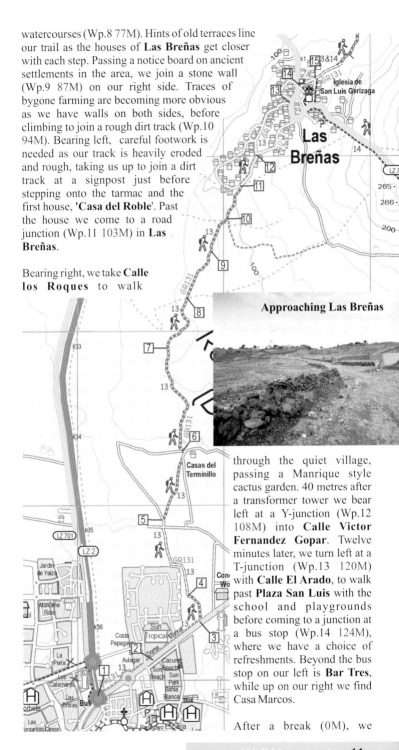

Approaching Las Breñas

through the quiet village, passing a Manrique style cactus garden. 40 metres after a transformer tower we bear left at a Y-junction (Wp.12 108M) into **Calle Victor Fernandez Gopar**. Twelve minutes later, we turn left at a T-junction (Wp.13 120M) with **Calle El Arado**, to walk past **Plaza San Luis** with the school and playgrounds before coming to a junction at a bus stop (Wp.14 124M), where we have a choice of refreshments. Beyond the bus stop on our left is **Bar Tres**, while up on our right we find Casa Marcos.

After a break (0M), we

continue from the bus stop junction up **Calle La Cancela** to a sharp dogleg bend where a dirt track goes off to our left (Wp.15 4M) by a GR signpost. Here we are joined by Walk 14. Taking to the track, we pass the village's last white house, before passing the wall of a farm. We are out on our own again, following the rough stone littered track as we pass an electricity pylon (Wp.16 12M), our track dwindling to a width of a walking trail. We cross several watercourses, our trail broadening again, before crossing a water-eroded gully with fine sand (Wp.17 20M) amongst neglected terraces. The track becomes smooth and well walkable for us to enjoy the splendid panorama ahead as we walk through another eroded sandy section.

A short gentle climb is followed by a descent from where we have views of the **La Finca** white farm, our next objective, now still far in the distance. A track from the right joins us before we cross a rough gully with cracked slabs of old concrete (Wp.18 29M), the remains of a paved trail. Our gritty track is now more comfortable until we pass a 20-metre long sandy section and get onto more stone-littered stretch with sections of bare rock, having ruined stone walls on our left.

Crossing a watercourse, then another one (Wp.19 38M) twenty metres left of a lava wall - quite a feature in the otherwise barren land - we walk down the fine gritty track, crossing a series of gullies. We come down into a depression where we join a dirt track (Wp.20 44M) to bear right; its surface is so smooth that we can stride out as we parallel an embankment of the LZ-701 road.

GR131 marker after Wp.21

Climbing gently, we cross the access track for the **La Finca** houses (Wp.21 57M) before coming to overlook Yaiza's western roundabout; a true road design art when viewed from above. Continuing on the dirt track as it curves around below **Montaña Cinta**, we come to the end of our Walk 12 route (Wp.22 77M), which we follow along to the wide stepped descent between two pillars (Wp.23 85M) leading down to the

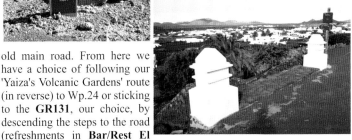

wide stepped descent Wp.23

old main road. From here we have a choice of following our 'Yaiza's Volcanic Gardens' route (in reverse) to Wp.24 or sticking to the **GR131**, our choice, by descending the steps to the road (refreshments in **Bar/Rest El Campo** opposite) before walking up the road, **Calle Vista de Yaiza**. Passing a bus stop, GR mapboard and art gallery we finish our route symbolically at **Bar Stop** by the church on **Plaza de los Remedios** (Wp.24 99M). A bus stop (along with a supermarket) is 200 metres ahead along the main street.

With the rash of waypMSosts planted by the authorities you might think they've got all the interesting walking covered - far from it, as we discover a beautiful airy walk that combines natural landscapes, thought-provoking art, and gastronomy in a route that nobody else seems to have discovered. Starting in **Yaiza**, we take an unlikely and rather unappealing exit from the town to reach the saddle below **Atalaya de Femés**, where we step out on a narrow donkey trail with elevated views. When the trail ends we have a modicum of road walking, enlivened by the house of a famous artist with its unusual alfresco artworks, followed by lunch at our favourite Lanzarote *típico*. Post refreshment, we leave **Las Breñas** on the **GR131**/Walk 13 to cross the *malpaís* to reach our final section where our gently elevated route gives us a new aspect over the lava fields and **Yaiza**.

In a nutshell it's a route that has just about everything you could hope for and at a low exertion rating. Note that **Casa Marcos** and **Los Tres** bar/restaurants in **Las Breñas** both close on Mondays. As 14kms might seem a bit long for a relaxed walk; our advice is to taxi from **Yaiza** to **La Degollada** which saves 3.2kms and the main ascent of 140 metres altitude.

| 3 | 3-3½ H | 14 km | 200m* / 200m* | ↻ | 5 |

*just 60 metres of ascents after **La Degollada**

Access by bus:
Service 60 **Arrecife/Playa Blanca** and 161 **Puerto del Carmen/Playa Blanca** serve **Yaiza**.

Access by car:
From the the LZ-2 take the roundabout exit for **Yaiza** to take the old main road into town. Drive to **Yaiza** church then turn south to park near the *ayuntamiento* offices and start of Walk 12 Yaiza Volcanic Gardens. Usually there's a local taxi parked here if you opt for a ride up to **La Degollada**.

From the old main road (Wp.1 0M) we walk south, the church on our left and *ayuntamiento* offices on our right to the start of our Walk 12 'Yaiza's Volcanic Gardens' route (Wp.2) where Walk 16 Atalaya de Femés Linear heads left (ESE) towards the main mountain. Our route is straight ahead (S then SW) on the main lane heading for **La Degollada**. There's not a lot to say about this section, a tarmac lane with little traffic, rising gently - surroundings a bit dull.

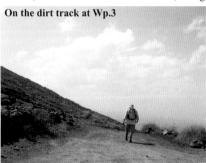

On the dirt track at Wp.3

Then it steepens quite dramatically as we approach the settlement.

We find ourselves in a 'huff and puff' steep tarmac ascent between the first, and rather cute, white houses with green detailing set amongst lava-walled cultivated black *picón* plots. Finally we come to the top of the lane to find ourselves on the saddle between the **Atalaya de Femés** and **Montaña El Cabo** (Wp.3 60M) - by this point you'll probably appreciate our suggestion of taking the **Yaiza** taxi to this location at the end of the tarmac. From the end of the tarmac, we continue on a dirt track that in fifty metres has shrunk to a narrow walking trail that contours (SW) along the hillside below the **Atalaya de Femés**. While our trail is narrow it is comfortable walking with superb

Superb views

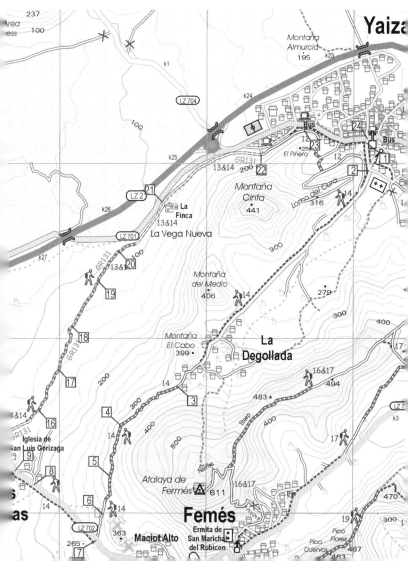

views over the **Janubio** lagoon and **Las Breñas** village from our elevated 300+ metres altitude. After climbing gently our path comes under lichen-covered lava boulders stacked dramatically above our route (Wp.4 72M), giving the impression they could fall at any moment - they haven't moved in years, after which the hillside takes on a less dramatic aspect as **Montaña Roja** and **Playa Blanca** come into hazy view across the southern plain.

Since the precarious lava boulders we've been following our contouring trail due south. Now, as the huge quarry at **Maciot Alto** starts to dominate the view, our trail starts dropping (Wp.5 79M), becoming narrower and pickier as our descent increases towards a roofed water reservoir. Carefully picking our way down the narrow trail, almost stepped in parts, we come onto the end of a jeep track and follow this (S) to pass the water reservoir on our right (Wp.6 85M) to come onto the reservoir's access track. It would be useful if a trail cut across to the **Las Breñas** road at this point, but rather than tackle open ground we walk along the access track to the LZ-703 **Las Breñas** road (Wp.7 89M), turn right and stroll down the left hand side, facing the occasional oncoming car, towards **Las Breñas**. We pass a barren football pitch on our left, where a gully is tunneled under the road, before arriving at the village name sign and first house (Wp.8 98M) **Casa de la Cabra Vieja** - literally 'House of the Old Goat' which possibly might be descriptive or humorous. Opposite, **Calle Las Toscas** - lined with newish villas - goes right off the LZ-703.

You don't need to be a culture vulture or a gourmand, though you'll get the opportunity to be both as we continue along the LZ-703 to the unusual sight of a house whose grounds are littered with art, including an oversized trowel dominating the house itself (Wp.9 101M). This is the winter home of Berlin based, internationally renowned, artist Dieter Noss whose works are often

The house at Wp.9

featured in **Yaiza**'s art gallery. In addition to his giant trowel you'll find (if he hasn't moved them) a giant wire coat hanger, a massive golden key, giant pick and plenty more in the garden. The next villa is also used for visiting artists. Please respect Dieter's privacy and restrict yourself to roadside viewing and pictures of this unique opportunity to be an art connoisseur.

Continuing down the road, we turn right onto **Calle La Cancela** (Wp.10) which we follow along above the church and **Casa Marcos** - unfortunately no direct access to these - to then go downhill to a sharp dogleg bend where we meet the **GR131**/Walk13 (Wp.15 107M) - note the jump in waypoint numbering to that used in Walk 13.

Our choice is to continue on the street (**GR131**) to come along to the main entrance to **Las Breñas** (Wp.14) where we have a choice of refreshments at **Los Tres** down on our right or **Casa Marcos** up on our left. After refreshment we follow the directions for Walk 13, including the waypoint numbers, for our return to **Yaiza** on the **GR131**.

This pleasant circular walk offers a surprising variety of landscapes. Starting in **Uga**, we turn into a valley of goat and camel farms, then a short climb across a mountain ridge separating animal farmlands from cultivation brings us to **Yaiza**, with a good choice of refreshments half-way into the route. On our return to **Uga** we skirt a stream of jagged lava, a petrified witness of the 18th century eruptions of **Timanfaya**, of which we enjoy good views during the final stage of our route. You may be sharing the route with camels, which use the section between Wp.11 to Wp.2 and Wp.2 to Wp.4 on their 6km trip to and from 'work' at the roadside of the LZ-67.

You can start the walk in **Yaiza**, bearing straight ahead at Wp.2 directly to the 'camel' tunnel, but if you want to pause for refreshments in **Uga**, turn left.

Access by car: Park in **Uga** near the church. On-street parking is between Wp.1 and 2, or you can park at the large car park at the *mercado*, south-east of the church. If you start the walk in **Yaiza**, you'll find parking 100 metres south-west of the church (Wp.9).

Access by bus: The 60 serves both **Yaiza** and **Uga** from **Arrecife/Playa Blanca**. The 161 serves **Yaiza** from **Puerto del Carmen/Playa Blanca**.

From the church in **Uga** (Wp.1 0M), we follow the broad street **Calle Joaquín Rodríguez** west, passing **Rest Casa Gregorio** before the road starts to ascend. Keeping straight ahead at junctions we come to a crossroads (Wp.2 8M), 30 metres before the main LZ-2 road. Our return route, **Camino de los Camellos**, is signed to the right as we turn left into a palm-lined alley signed 'Solo paso de camellos'. These signs say it all about who are the most frequent users of the track and passageway.

The alleyway takes us through a tunnel under the LZ-2 to come to a junction

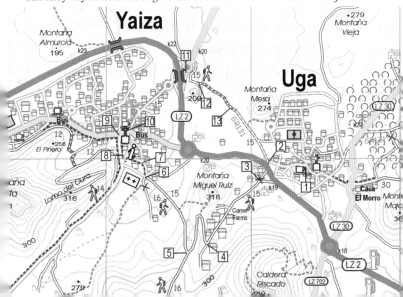

(Wp.3 11M). Bearing right, we are on a substantial tarmac lane, **Camino Vallito de Uga**, lined by villas and an abundance of farmsteads. Tarmac gives way to dirt as we walk deeper into the valley, animal farms lining our route before passing a quarry on our left. 60 metres after the quarry, we turn right on an ascending track (Wp.4 26M) before shabby white buildings.

ruined molino at Wp.5

Leaving the valley with its farmlands scent behind us, our track swings north as we climb, views of **Timanfaya** gradually expanding as we gain elevation. After the left hairpin bend (S) we join the fence of a goat farm and see **Yaiza**. Gently climbing along the track brings us to a junction at the ruined *molino* (Wp.5 42M), the high point of our route.

The track to our left continues up the mountain, but we swing around the old mill (N) enjoying views of **Yaiza** as we descend. The track takes us down between fields and vineyards. We reach first houses and step onto tarmac to bear right 40 metres later at a junction (Wp.6 57M) just before **La Casona de Yaiza** and follow **Calle Barranco de la Molina**. After 150 metres we turn left into **Calle la Tahona** (Wp.7 59M).

We pass a mansion followed by a small park on our left, then keep straight on at a crossroads before bearing right (Wp.8 63M) at a junction, skirting a large community plaza. Past a restaurant, the post office and playground we come to the church at **Plaza de los Remedios** (Wp.9 67M), a good place to take a break with a few bars on hand.

Taking the pavement (0M) along the road (E), we pass bars and a minimarket before coming to a junction at **Centro de Artesanía** (Wp.10 2M), where we veer left (NE), following signs for '**Tinajo/Timanfaya**'. We are on **Calle Montañas del Fuego**, our road passing the Guardia Civil and a petrol station as we walk out of the village. Straight on at a roundabout, we pass under the LZ-2 bridge to come to a roundabout, where just after the right-hand slip road, we find a GR signpost and a tarmac lane (Wp.11 17M). Turning sharp right we take the lane and start to flank a field of lava. The tarmac soon gives up, our dirt track swinging left before a house. As we are about to pass a 'Caminos Naturales' mapboard, we are caught up by an unexpected party - a long caravan of camels on their way to the farm at **Vallito de Uga**! Amused by the unusual scenery, we give the caravana right of way before resuming our walk, bearing left at a Y-junction of tracks (Wp.12 21M), the right branch leading to a private property.

Our track then dwindles to a trail as we head SE to pass another 'Caminos Naturales' mapboard, after which we ignore a track to the left when our trail becomes a track and joins a long fence (Wp.13 29M). Maintaining direction (SE), we follow the track alongside vineyards, ignoring all left hand branches we simply shadow the fence back to the crossroads at Wp.2 (42M). Turning left, we return to our starting point at the church (50M).

Femés remains our favourite Lanzarote village. While we have the option of driving into the village and ascending the **Atalaya** by our unique circular route, we recognise that bus travellers and classicists like the traditional linear route. This is a long energetic ascent, as after the first kilometre every step is upwards until we reach the antennaed summit, from where we have a choice of returning by the same route to our start point or descending to **Femés**; our preference. Then to return to your start, we suggest our '**Atalaya de Femés - CircularRoute**', until you meet up with your outward route.

While this is one of the island's wilder routes, wayfinding is very straightforward. Virtually all the route is on clear tracks and paths, and if you do have any navigation questions, the answer is always 'uphill'.

*Distances are **Yaiza/Uga** - **Atalaya** 7 kilometres, **Atalaya** - **Femés** 2.7 kilometres, **Femés** - **Yaiza/Uga** 6.2 kilometres using the 'Circular' route.

Access by bus:
Route Nº5 operates a limited **Arrecife** - **Femés** service Monday to Friday but you'll need to get up early. 60 and 161 services stop at **Yaiza** church on the old main road, or entrance to **Uga**.

Access by car:
Park in the car park near the church in **Yaiza**.

Starting from **Yaiza**.
From outside the church (Wp.1 0M) we walk away from the old main road passing public buildings on each side; note the Cultura y Educación office on the left; to pass a large public square on our left and come to the junction at the top of the square (Wp.2). Ahead the road runs on to **La Degollada**, while on our front right are the **Volcanic Gardens**, built to commemorate the 250th anniversary of the **Timanfaya** eruption.

From Wp.2, we follow the wide road left (ESE). When the tarmac changes to black *picón* grit (Wp.3), take a break to look up; our eyes are drawn to the massive *lomo* rising up to the **Atalaya** peak, it looks big and distant - both are true, but don't be daunted in your quest. We have easy striding across a plain before the track starts climbing, steadily at first but then steeper as a 'puff and grunt' ascent up to a junction by a giant tooth (Wp.4), once a complete windmill but seemingly more diminished each time we pass.

Starting from Uga
We start from opposite the village road junction with one of those quirky Spanish road junctions where you go right then attempt to cross the busy traffic to go right, instead of the logical turn left lane; see map. If you get off the bus at the church walk out past **Bar Gregorio** then left, right, left and up to carefully cross the main road.

From the southern side of the junction a dirt road leads up around a large house

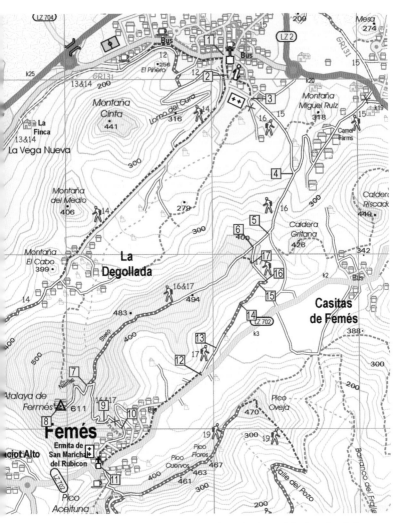

to a junction where the left hand track is 'Solo Camels'! Keeping left, we come onto a fertile plain after which our track runs along a valley floor as the ridges rise on each side of our route.

Stark farm buildings, including camel farms, line the track until we come to a track off to the right heading toward a huge molar on the ridge above us. We turn up the track to climb up to a saddle and then up the line of the ridge to pass the remains of the old windmill and join our **Yaiza** route (Wp.4).

There's plenty of uphill ahead, so you might want to take a first break on the windmill saddle, with views west across the **Valle de Fena** to the **Volcanic Gardens** and east down over the rather scruffy camel farms, before tackling the serious ascent ahead.

Combined Route

From the 'tooth', our black *picón* track runs straight up the spine in a steady ascent. When the black track goes down towards the **Femés** valley (Wp.5) we keep right on a rocky track, and then keep right at a second cairned track (Wp.6) which leads down into the valley, our return route. We keep right and uphill at these junctions with the **Atalaya** coming into view ahead. Surprisingly, we have a small downhill section before the ascent is rejoined, sections of **Femés** coming into sight along with views over the scattered houses and plots of **La Degollada**.

Our steady ascent brings us up onto a plateau on the wide ridge and for once the walking becomes an easy stroll as we saunter past rocky outcrops which provide enough moisture and shelter for plant life to thrive, in contrast to the barren landscape we've been walking through.

After skirting the outcrops, and with the peak's aerials ahead, our track dwindles to a path across a narrow section of the ridge and a small descent before we face a stiff 'puff and grunt' climb. The steep climb - stairs cut in the trail would be most useful - brings us up onto a trackless plateau where cairns guide us front left over to the start of a faint track which takes us onto the **Atalaya**'s access road (Wp.7).

Once on the broad dirt road navigation, which has not been at all difficult to this point, becomes simplicity itself. We head up the broad track climbing up through a zigzag to look down into a 'named' *caldera*. It's then a straight uphill slog to the peak's trig point (Wp.8) beside the buildings and aerials.

At the far end of the buildings we find a stepped path leading down to a cave house, just the place to take off your backpack and relax. The two small rooms and plastered walls appear to pre-date the transmitters, and a path leads on to a second smaller cave also shaped for habitation.

Descent to Femés

From the trig point, **Femés** village square looks both inviting and deceptively close. Our descent is so straightforward (we just head down the access track) that no description is necessary except to say, take care. The track is eroded in places and has a loose grit/dust surface in others making for a skittery descent with the possibility of being unceremoniously dumped on your bottom; we know!

... the 'named' *caldera* between Wps. 7&8

We pass our upward route (Wp.7 8M) and after a series of zig-zags we pass a track going steeply down to our right (Wp.9). After the chained vehicle barrier (30M) we come onto a village dirt road (Wp.10) to go right and pass the bottom of the track we saw earlier. Reaching the village houses, we come onto tarmac/concrete streets where keeping straight ahead brings us into the village square and **Bar Femés** (Wp.11).

On the peak

Return to Yaiza/Uga

Now, most walkers climb back up the access road to walk back down the ridge to their start point but unless you are a deliberate masochist who enjoys uphill climbs, then why not try something a little bit different with the start of our **Atalaya de Femés - Circular** route? It is certainly easier than the access road, and does mean that you are not repeating yourself.

We start out from **Bar Femés** (Wp.11 0M) by walking down the road (NE) away from the village. As the pavement ends (5M) we keep to the main road passing the lower section of the village on our left as easy strolling takes us down past a decorative palm garden before we come to a dirt track (Wp.12, 19M). We take the track to come above black *picón* fields and a hut (Wp.13 25M) just before the track runs out (28M) for us to come onto a narrow walking trail running behind the northern edge of the fields. A white painted cairn marks a small gully (Wp.14), cairns ahead of us marking our trail's route to climb up onto a spur of the main ridge. Across an affluent and the trail is less distinct, as we ascend from the corner of the last field (Wp.15) to cross another affluent.

Across two more affluents in this furrowed landscape and we're climbing the cairned path, the final cairn (Wp.16) appearing as a 'head & shoulders' from lower down the trail. A final climb brings us onto a broad *lomo* running south-east from the main ridge, with views to **Puerto del Carmen**. Now we start climbing in earnest. A faint track leads us up the *lomo* in a slogging ascent over the barren ground. Onwards and upwards we come to a faint junction (Wp.17) where we keep right to connect with our outward route. From here it's all downhill to the windmill 'tooth', where it is down left for **Yaiza**, or onwards and down right for **Uga**.

Traditionally, the route up to the **Atalaya de Femés** is a linear one from either **Yaiza** or **Uga**, described in detail in our 'Atalaya de Femés - Linear Walk' description. **Femés** is a beautiful village nestling in a fold at the top of the escarpment overlooking the **Rubicón** plain, easiest to reach by hire car but also accessible by bus. So here is our circular route up the **Atalaya**, definitely both the simplest and most interesting way of taking in the peak.

Access by car: There's plenty of parking around **Femés** village square.

Access by bus: N°5 **Arrecife** to **Femés** leaves at 8:15 & 14:10 weekdays only, returning from the village at 15:00 and 20:00. Check these times have not been changed!

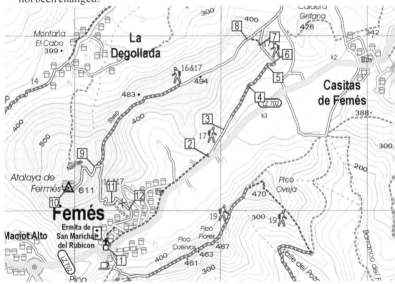

We start out from **Bar Femés** (Wp.1 0M 373 metres, closed Thursdays) by walking down the road (NE) away from the village - yes, we're walking away from the mountain that we intend to climb. This seems more than a little crazy, but bear with us. As the pavement ends (5M) we keep to the main road passing the lower section of the village on our left as we come to a bus shelter (12M). More easy strolling takes us down past a decorative palm garden before we come to a dirt track (Wp.2 19M). At last we leave the tarmac, taking to the track to come above black *picón* fields and a hut (Wp.3 25M) just before the track runs out (28M) and we come onto a narrow walking trail running behind the northern edge of the fields.

A white painted cairn marks a small gully (Wp.4), cairns ahead of us marking our trail's route to climb up onto a spur of the main ridge. Across an affluent, the trail becomes less distinct as we ascend from the corner of the last field (Wp.5) to cross another affluent. Across another two affluents in this furrowed landscape, and we are climbing the cairned path, the final cairn (Wp.6 44M) resembling a 'head & shoulders' from lower down the trail. A final climb brings us onto a broad *lomo* running south-east from the main ridge, with views over to **Puerto del Carmen**.

Now we start climbing in earnest. A faint track leads us up the *lomo* in a slogging ascent over barren ground. Onwards and upwards, we come to a faint junction (Wp.7). We keep straight ahead, the track dwindling to nothing as we cross the rock-littered open ground before coming onto the clear track of our linear route running up the *lomo* (Wp.8 61M). Our steady ascent brings us onto a plateau on the wide ridge; for once the walking becomes an easy stroll as we saunter past rocky outcrops which provide sufficient moisture and shelter for plant life to thrive, in contrast to the barren landscape we have been walking through. After skirting the outcrops, and with the peak's aerials ahead, our track dwindles to a path across a narrow section of the ridge and a small descent before we face a stiff 'puff and grunt' climb. The steep climb - stairs cut in the trail would be most useful - brings us up onto a trackless plateau where cairns guide us front left over to the start of a faint track which takes us onto the **Atalaya**'s access road (Wp.9 98M).

Once on the broad dirt road navigation, which has not been at all difficult to this point, becomes simplicity itself. We head up the broad track climbing up through a zigzag to look down into a 'named' *caldera* and then straight uphill slog to the peak's trig point (Wp.10 107M) beside the buildings and aerials. Going to the far end of the buildings we find a stepped path leading down to a cave house; just the place to take off your backpack and relax. The two small rooms and plastered walls appear to predate the transmitters, and a path leads on to a second smaller cave also shaped for habitation.

Descent to Femés

Descent to Femés

From the trig point (Wp.10 0M), **Femés** village square looks both inviting and deceptively close. Our descent is so straightforward (we just head down the access track) that no description is necessary except to say, take care. The track is eroded in places and has a loose grit/dust surface in others making for a skittery descent with the possibility of being unceremoniously dumped on your bottom; we know!

We pass our upward route (Wp.9 8M) and after a series of zig-zags we pass a track going steeply down to our right (Wp.11 23M). After the chained vehicle barrier we come onto a village dirt road (Wp.12 32M) to go right and pass the bottom of the track we saw earlier. Reaching the village houses, we come onto tarmac/concrete streets where keeping straight ahead brings us into the village square and **Bar Femés** (Wp.1 42M) with more scenically positioned refreshments available a short stroll away on the edge of the **Femés** escarpment.

18 The Hidden Barrancos

Safe from the depredations of tourism is a region of barren grandeur comprising the **Higuera** and **Casita** *barrancos*. When we discovered this route it was little-known, though it's now become relatively popular with energetic walkers. The only development since we first walked the route consists of a basic refuge near its half way point. It might be called a refuge but it offers negligible shade, so set out well protected and with plenty of water for this adventure in the wilderness. Clear paths make for easy route finding, with the exception of finding our outward path by the goat farm.

Access by car: park in **Femés**.

Short Walk
Follow the route in reverse to ascend **Pico Aceituna** and return the same way. 1.5 hours, 4 kilometres, 200 metres ascents/descents.

Access by bus:
N°5 **Arrecife** to **Femés,** see Walk 17 for details.

Across the 'main' road from **Bar Femés** we start out on a tarmac lane (Wp.1 0M 376 metres) heading south (S) towards a ridge topped with an ugly farm. The tarmac soon gives way to dirt as we start a slogging ascent up towards the farm, passing two paths on our right before struggling up to the end of the track beside the goat farm on the ridge (Wp.2 7M) to look down into the **Barranco de la Higuera**. Here the ground is churned up by the goats which can confuse the confuse-able as to where the path is. Keeping the main farm

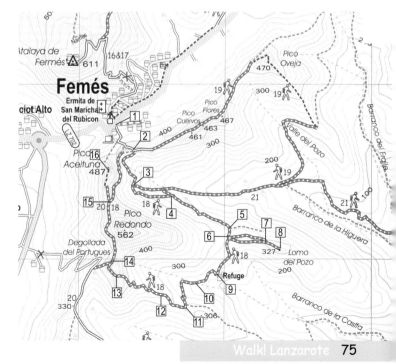

and corral on our left, we step to the edge of the ridge.

Away on our right is our return path, clearly outlined against the rock, while below us our dusty narrow path drops down into the *barranco*. It is a skittery descent on the loose, goat-churned surface, dropping past multi-hued

Walking signs and goats on top of the ridge

The start of the descent

rocks to turn below **Pico Aceituna** (and the return path) to start a zigzag descent down to a cobbled section (18M).

Now we are on an undulating easy section of path which heads towards an electricity pylon, **Puerto Calero** coming into view in the distance. We wind steadily downhill, passing Nicotiana plants struggling to survive in this barren landscape.

Passing a path to our left (Wp.3 27M) (our original route, and an option to finish in **Playa Quemada**) we start turning into and out of the affluents which feed the main *barranco* before we come under the pylon to step onto an old jeep track (30M). A path connects sections of the old track as we follow the line of the pylons; ahead we can see our trail's extension as we pass a path coming up from our left (Wp.4, our original route) before coming down to a second pylon.

From the pylon, we ignore traces heading into the *barranco* as we start heading up the main path which climbs up past a crumbling corral and crossing an affluent before a slogging ascent brings us up past great swathes of Asphodels to meet the ridge's crest at a broad saddle.

On reaching the saddle we find a wide stone-littered plain, on our left is another trace/path down to **Playa Quemada** (Wp.5) while our route continues ahead as a swept path through the rock litter. An easy stroll takes us over to a junction (Wp.6 55M) where a jeep track and a path head left (E) to the small peak of **Morro de Lomo del Pozo**.

Having come this far it would be foolish to ignore the extension to the *morro* (literally, the snout or nose) so we head out on the narrow path, an easy stroll until we close with the peak where the gradient increases by the first outcrop. The jeep track comes up to join us (Wp.7) - not that you'd want to drive anything on this track - for a steep ascent up to a pair of large cairns which mark the summit (Wp.8 66M). We return to the junction (Wp.6 80M) on the jeep track.

Back on the main route, we head SW on the path, the refuge coming into sight like a mirage in this barren expanse. Our path heads down through an affluent to bring us to the refuge (Wp.9 86M), perched on the edge of the **Barranco de la Casita**.

We give thanks to the authorities who have constructed a refuge in the middle

Relaxing at the refuge

of nowhere, and honour the construction with our presence for a break; if only they had put a proper roof on it to provide some meaningful shade.

Relaxing at the refuge, we can appreciate the subtle variations of the rock hues in this arid environment, as well as contemplating the task ahead of us as we sit under the looming presence of **Pico Redondo**.

From the refuge (0M) we follow the path as it winds down into a gully, after which our path unwinds along the side of the big *barranco*, crossing a couple of affluents before coming into the ravine proper to run down to cross the line of the watercourse (Wp.10). Standing on the *barranco* floor, we appreciate that the next stage is of necessity energetic. All around us the land rises up to high ridges and to **Pico Redondo**, none of it vertical but all of it muscle-sapping steep. Looking up the ravine we can see our next objective, the high saddle to the left of **Pico Redondo**, and very high up it appears from this viewpoint.

Our broad path angles up the southern slope before swinging left for a long traverse up onto the ridge which separates us from **Barranco de los Dises**, a 'puff and grunt' ascent up through zigzags bringing us onto the ridge by an old corral (Wp.11 17M 295 metres) to look longingly back to the refuge. Now our path heads straight up the ridge, getting rougher as we come up to pass a rocky peak thick with asphodels (Wp.12 343 metres).

Ahead, our path zigzags up a steeper section of the *lomo*, yet another 'puff and grunt' ascent, taking breaks at each turn. This relentless slog up the *lomo* is brightened by the flocks of goats of all shades and sizes that we always find on this ridge. The goats are not quite pettable but give a bemused look at us strange bipeds who make such hard work of the rocky ground that they simply skip over.

... bemused goats ...

Eventually our ascent brings

us up onto the saddle between **Pico Redondo** and **Hacha Grande** (Wp.13 48M 449 metres).

From the saddle, a narrow path curves right around the peak's western slopes to bring us above a goat farm set on a saddle fifty metres below us. We come down to a path junction (Wp.14 52M) where our 'Femés-Playa Blanca' route goes down to the farm and dirt road. Keeping right, our narrow path, and a black water pipe, curve round a steep bowl (possibly vertiginous for some) past bands of soft hued rock before a short ascent takes us over a spur into a smaller bowl. **Pico Aceituna** is ahead as we come up past deep purple rock to emerge onto the saddle between **Redondo** and **Aceituna** (Wp.15 72M).

Here we take a diversion off the main route to climb **Pico Aceituna**. A faint path leads up the lower slopes but soon disappears amongst the rocks. We simply keep climbing straight up, picking our steps over the rocks to come onto the summit (Wp.16) beside a large stone corral which has been built in this least likely location. From the northern end of the peak we look down on **Femés**, while the views over the **Rubicón** plain to **Playa Blanca** and Fuerteventura are a fitting reward for this small ascent.

It is possible to scramble down the northern face of the peak - possible, but not recommended, and so we retrace our upward route back to the saddle (Wp.15). We leave the saddle on a narrow path dropping down into the **Barranco de la Higuera**, our route curving round beneath **Aceituna** before climbing up to the goat farm ridge by a second building. We take a path down the slope in front of the building to join the dirt road for a relaxed stroll down to the village centre, where a choice of refreshment opportunities should not be overlooked; **Bar Femés** is closest and least touristy but also the least picturesque.

Femés is a favourite with us. Way back in 1995, our 'Hidden Barrancos' route pioneered walking in the **Higuera** and **Casita** *barrancos*, our route now appearing in other books and our subsequent routes being the basis of the new wayposting in this previously neglected region.

Femés Ridge is one of the few Lanzarote routes where you get close to a high mountain feeling, yet we reach the mountain peak in a relatively relaxed manner on a little-known path, plus some open ground climbing. We have magnificent views from **Pico Oveja** (Sheep Peak) over the southern peaks, before descending into the valleys. You cannot get that high - and that low - on a circular route, without the inevitable uphill finish; a long slog up through the old Majo settlement in the **Barranco de la Higuera**. Quite simply, a modern classic route for experienced walkers.

Access by car:
Park in the centre of **Femés** near the church square.

Access by bus:
N°5 **Arrecife** to **Femés,** see Walk 17 for details.

Short Walk
To **Pico Oveja** and return (3 Walker, 1¾ hours).

Heading up the track at the start

From **Bar Femés** (Wp.1 0M) we cross the main road to head up the track, tarmac soon giving way to dirt, towards the ugly goat farm sat on the ridge. The slogging ascent up between the water tanks and past a trail off to our right brings us up to the farm's modern door entrance (Wp.2 7M), where we continue along the track (E) to head over a crest to a second farm (Wp.3 12M) with noisy chained dogs.

The track ends as we continue on the northern side of the ridge following a trail - really a mere trace of a goat trail - to maintain height as we head towards the first of the peaks. When one trace finishes we simply step onto another, a path gradually emerging as we come below the first peak (Wp.4), a rocky scramble if you want to take in the views.

Looking back at Femés from the ridge

Black *picón* fields dot the **Femés Valley** below us, while ahead in the distance are the

Timanfaya Fire Mountains (**Montañas del Fuego**), but no views south until the rocky ridge runs down to a 'rock free' crest where we step up from the path to marvel at the southern landscapes.

Timanfaya Fire Mountains ahead

Back on the path, we maintain height until our path starts running downhill to a saddle, the surface becoming rock-littered, slowing our progress before disappearing entirely in a maze of goat traces. From the saddle, we climb up to a boulder-mounted cairn on the ridge (Wp.5 28M) for more breathtaking views into the valleys.

From the cairn, we continue along the ridge saddle past a pair of *zoco* style small corrals, a faint path emerging as the ridge rises again on our right to **Pico Oveja**. Maintaining height, we see ahead that our current trail runs down, becoming more defined as it descends to meet a trail from **Casitas de Femés** on a broad saddle.

Now it's decision time. We could continue on the improving trail across the northern slopes of **Pico Oveja** and the ridge line before turning back into the 'hidden barrancos', all of it easy walking on defined trails (see map section); or we could head direct for the peak, a rather more adventurous option.

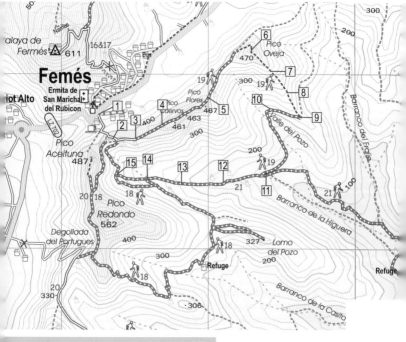

Being adventurous, we go uphill over open ground and goat traces, aiming for an old terrace; there are a few of these small boulder-supported terraces, but simply head for the highest one. Continuing diagonally uphill towards the line of the ridge, we cross another terrace before coming up to a low stone wall which runs up the ridge. Now we follow the wall until it gives out, from where a 'puff and grunt' ascent brings us up to **Pico Oveja** (Wp.6 55M).

Stepping around the peak itself, we move from a comparatively gentle landscape to an orogenical one. After that climb it would be a waste to immediately strike off down into the valleys, and even though there is plenty **Wonderful views fromPico Oveja** of proof that the peak is popular with goats, we find some suitable ledges at a comfortable height on the southern side, on which to be seated while taking in the views.

From our vantage point on the peak we can see the trail coming over the saddle from **Casitas de Femés**, our first objective on the descent.

This is pathless country with a picky descent, steep in places before we reach the path, so if in doubt, return by our outward route to **Femés** or backtrack to the alternative path.

We strike off from the peak (0M) along the line of the ridge (SE) carefully picking our way down to where the ridge broadens into a rock-littered *lomo*. Keeping direction (SE), we stroll down the *lomo*, surrounded by superb views, to its 'nose' (Wp.7). The steep 'nose' calls for care as we pick our way down over loose rock and boulders. Taking a break on this picky descent we can see the trail from **Casitas** coming over a saddle, still a long way ahead and down from our position.

At the base of the 'nose' we look back at the line of our descent - it looks almost sheer from below (!), before resuming a strolling descent of the rock-littered *lomo* to pass the remains of a corral (Wp.8) and finally come down to the trail (Wp.9 36M), positively a 'walking motorway' in these pathless expanses. From here you could turn left for **Casitas** and return to **Femés** on the road, an easier but less spectacular route than what we have ahead. Once on the path, we follow it right, our route feeling comfortably luxuríous after the *lomo*, to start dropping (NW) into the **Valle del Pozo**.

After heading up the valley and gradually descending, we come down to cross a water runoff by an old stone wall (Wp.10 41M). Across the runoff, our trail swings left (SSE) down towards the main valley and a line of small electricity pylons.

Our faint path crosses another runoff and follows old stone walls, this section giving a wonderful sense of spaciousness as we stroll down to cross more runoffs before swinging right (SSW) into the main valley where we come alongside a jeep track, which our path joins by an electricity pylon (Wp.11 52M).

We've been descending continuously for nearly an hour, and now we face the consequences in the form of a long uphill slog along the **Barranco de la Higuera**. Setting off from the pylon we follow the jeep track beside the broad water runoff. As we climb this relentless ascent, we start to pass old corrals and stone walls before crossing the runoff (Wp.12) which now becomes a small gorge on our right. Technically, the jeep track should be an easy section of our route, but it doesn't feel like it as we labour up past pylons, corrals and stone walls before crossing an affluent (Wp.13) which brings the hideous goat farms into view high up on the ridge ahead; and before you ask the answer is, 'Yes, we *do* have to climb up there!'.

The remains of corrals and buildings litter the valley floor, some thought to be remains of Majo settlements (the eastern Canary Islands' equivalent of the western islands' Guanches), pre-dating the Spanish invasion. A second division of this agricultural settlement was based around the mouth of the *barranco* at **Playa del Pozo**. There have been some archaeological investigations made of these ruins; their Majo heritage seems well proven.

We keep slogging up the rough jeep track, passing a trail off to our left (our original route in 'The Hidden Barrancos') (Wp.14) and crossing an affluent where the track swings up to our left and we continue ahead on a clear trail.

The path junction at 94 minutes

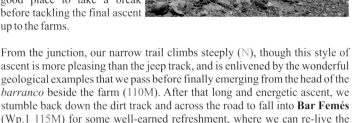

This trail climbs steeply up to join our 'Hidden Barrancos' route at a path junction (Wp.15 94M) which provides us with a good place to take a break before tackling the final ascent up to the farms.

From the junction, our narrow trail climbs steeply (N), though this style of ascent is more pleasing than the jeep track, and is enlivened by the wonderful geological examples that we pass before finally emerging from the head of the *barranco* beside the farm (110M). After that long and energetic ascent, we stumble back down the dirt track and across the road to fall into **Bar Femés** (Wp.1 115M) for some well-earned refreshment, where we can re-live the wonders of this modern classic that we've just completed.

The long route out of **Playa Blanca** via **Papagayo Beach** and up the dirt track to the **Degollada del Portugués**, followed by path and track into **Femés**, is one of Lanzarote's classic long distance routes. As with many of the island's long linear routes, accessibility is a problem. After an initial climb out of **Femés** we skirt around **Pico Aceituna** on our 'Hidden Barrancos' route in reverse, before dropping down to the **Degollada del Portugués**. From this pass, we stroll down a dirt track to emerge from the mountains onto the far south of the **Rubicón** desert plain. Our official route then wanders along the coast, with the opportunity of testing the famous beaches of this region, before heading into **Playa Blanca** on the return route of Walk 9 and the coastal promenade to reach the 'old town'.

Access from Playa Blanca: taxi to **Femés**.

Access by bus: N°5 **Arrecife-Femés** leaves at 8:15 Mondays to Fridays only; you should reach **Bar Femés** at approximately 09.00. N°60 services back from **Playa Blanca** to **Arrecife**.

Access by car: drive to **Femés**, and park by the village square and taxi back from **Playa Blanca**.
2CSK Route though make sure you start from **Femés** end of the route. Park the lower car as described for Walk 9 '**Papagayo Beach**', and reduce distance to 19 kilometres. Or, pay the access fee and park at **Papagayo Beach** parking; reduce distance to 16 kilometres.

Fine views on the descent

We start out from **Bar Femés** (Wp.1 0M); if you're walking our routes in order, you'll be a well-known regular in this little bar by now. Following Walks 18 & 19 up onto the ridge, we then take Walk 18 in reverse (Wp.2 11M) to come onto the pass between **Pico Aceituna** and **Pico Redondo** (Wp.3 24M).

The path below **Pico Redondo** is a little trickier, and might cause vertigo sufferers a little trouble, before reaching the path junction (Wp.4) above the goat farm, where we follow the black water pipe down past the farm and onto the **Degollada del Portugués** (Wp.5 43M).

A track, barred to vehicle access, climbs up from the **Rubicón** desert plain through a series of zigzags before crossing the *degollada* to run down the **Barranco de los Dises**. We stroll down the track, passing another *degollada* viewpoint at the head of the *barranco* before coming under the bulk of **Hacha Grande** to snake in and out of sharp clefts in the mountain.

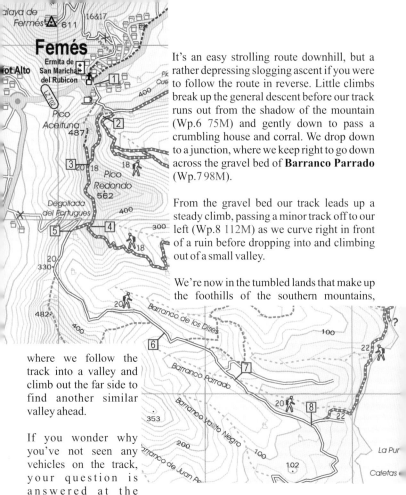

It's an easy strolling route downhill, but a rather depressing slogging ascent if you were to follow the route in reverse. Little climbs break up the general descent before our track runs out from the shadow of the mountain (Wp.6 75M) and gently down to pass a crumbling house and corral. We drop down to a junction, where we keep right to go down across the gravel bed of **Barranco Parrado** (Wp.7 98M).

From the gravel bed our track leads up a steady climb, passing a minor track off to our left (Wp.8 112M) as we curve right in front of a ruin before dropping into and climbing out of a small valley.

We're now in the tumbled lands that make up the foothills of the southern mountains, where we follow the track into a valley and climb out the far side to find another similar valley ahead.

If you wonder why you've not seen any vehicles on the track, your question is answered at the notoríous 'suzuki trap' (Wp.9 144M) where the water runoff effectively seals the route to all but the toughest all-wheel drive vehicles. There still plenty of runoffs to cross before we come to the last one (Wp.10 189M) where a final climb-out brings us onto the edge of the **Rubicón** desert plain at a track junction (Wp.11 197M).

From the foot of the mountains we look out over the hazy plain to the headland bar above **Papagayo Beach** and the white scars that are the eastern outskirts of **Playa Blanca**, and we have a problem. Until now, wayfinding has simply meant keeping to the main track, but now we have a plethora of tracks and trails to choose from with few identifiable landmarks to guide us. If you want the quickest way to the bar, then follow a track WSW and then forking S to come onto the main track serving the **Papagayo** parking area.

Our scenic route goes SE on a track and then follow coastal paths - plenty to choose from, to either drop into beaches such as **El Pasito** (a strange glitch caused us to lose our GPS track at this point; possibly distracted by naturists, we forgot to power up after taking a break on the beach), or pass above the bays where possible.

Our final objective, Playa Blanca, is in sight

Our scenic route is a bit longer in distance and time for us to arrive at the **Papagayo** bars (Wp.12 253M) a few minutes behind those taking the shorter dirt track alternative.

From **Papagayo** we follow Walk 9 back to the road system below the **Papagayo Arena Hotel** (1.5 km 45M). On the roads follow the blue 'Papagayo Beach' signs in reverse down to a small roundabout, and then on walkways down to the pebble beach of **Playa del Afe**; you could reach this point by staying to seaward of the hotel, and descending on paths directly onto the beach.

From the end of the beach, the coastal promenade starts, guiding us into the centre of **Playa Blanca** at the 'old town' (4 kilometres +60M).

By the time you've finished six hours of continuous hiking, you've certainly earned some reward for your efforts, and we bet you'll be glad you chose the 'downhill' option!

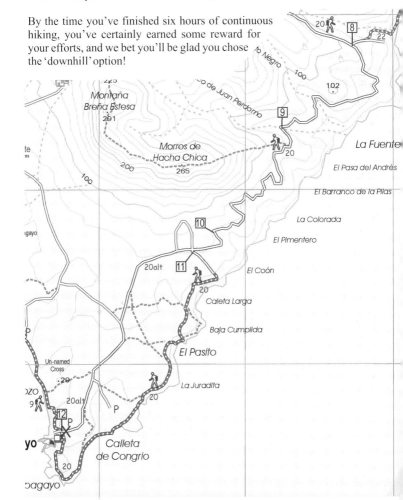

A very pleasant linear route from **Femés** to **Playa Quemada** to add to our repertoire of routes in this region. After the ascent up to the goat farm ridge, it's all downhill along the **Barranco de la Higuera** to **Playa del Pozo** then a final section on the tracks and trails of our 'Playa del Pozo' (Walk 22) route to finish in **Playa Quemada**.

There's a slight risk of vertigo in the early stages of the route . We've kept our description to a minimum as once you are past the goat farm, trail finding is easy - you don't want your head in a book when you have an easy walking route through impressive scenery to enjoy.

Access by bus:
N°60 **Arrecife** or **Playa Blanca** to **Yaiza and** N°161 from **Puerto del** **Carmen** to **Yaiza** and **Playa Blanca** then taxi to **Femés**. N°5 **Arrecife** to **Femés** leaves at 8:15 & 14:10 Mondays to Fridays only. Bus users will need to continue along the coast on Walk 2 to **Puerto Calero** for the water bus to **Puerto del Carmen**.

Access by car:
Park either by the square in **Femés** or in **Playa Quemada** near where the road swings right by the first restaurant. Unless you are using 2CSK you will have to re-walk the route to get back to your car; so it's probably best to start in **Playa Quemada** - then you get an easy return after lunch.

It's our usual start after coffee at **Bar Femés** (Wp.1 0M) to climb up the track to the ugly goat farm from where we take the 'Hidden Barrancos' trail (Wp.2 9M) down into the head of the **Barranco de la Higuera**.

Dropping swiftly down below **Pico Aceituna**, we come to the path junction (Wp.3 16M) to go left down the *barranco* on our 'Femés Ridge' route in reverse, a much easier option than the ascent on Walk 19. An easy strolling

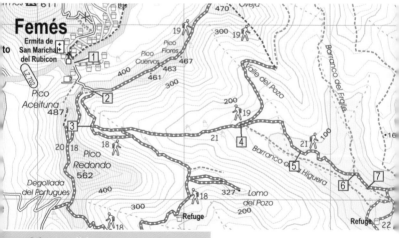

descent takes us down past the remains of *Majo* (*Guanche*) settlements to the pylon path junction (Wp.4 39M) where our 'Femés Ridge' route comes in from the **Valle del Pozo**.

Keeping to the jeep track, we move away from the line of the water runoff in the *barranco* (E) until we meet the runoff from **Valle del Pozo** to swing right (SSE) towards **Playa del Pozo**. We come back to the **Barranco de la Higuera** runoff (Wp.5 50M) to head down the broad valley, crossing the mouth of **Barranco del Fraile** (Wp.6 63M) to come to the track climbing up the eastern wall (Wp.7). Now we're on our 'Playa del Pozo' route, leaving the track to go onto the walking trail (Wp.8).

When we come to a lower path below us on our right we have a choice of following the main path on the inland route (Wp.9) or of following the lower path across the headlands and *barrancos* (Wp.10), both routes coming together again before we come to the outskirts of the **Playa Quemada** settlement (Wp.11 95M). Rather than follow the roads, we take the coastal path across to the sea front houses and restaurant (Wp.12 105M).

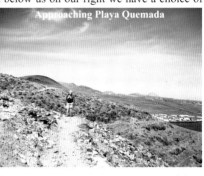
Approaching Playa Quemada

Extension to Puerto Calero (add 35 mins and 1.8km)
Our finish is already on the route of Walk 2; we simply continue east on the little access road. As we climb up to the last houses, **Puerto Calero** marina comes into view. Taking the coastal path from the end of housing, we follow Walk 2 in reverse onto the promenade, as far as the marina entrance where we turn left up the road to the bus stop by the roundabout (Bus Nº161), or turn right down into the marina to catch the water-bus to **Puerto del Carmen**.

Playa Quemada is literally the end of the road, but this doesn't mean that it's the end of exploring - far from it. Sections of this coastal exploration route get quite busy in a rather bizarre fashion, as the many people who head for the **Playa de la Arena** beach clad in the most minimalist gear contrast wildly with the *parapentistas* who labour up to their launch point with enormous back packs. Once away from the first section of the route you're into barren tranquility, strolling above the cliffs before dropping into the large **Barranco de la Higuera** to find a few cozzie-optional hikers enjoying the isolated beach of **Playa del Pozo** from where you can return if opting for a shorter version. We continue further on to discover the intriguing **Secret Garden** with the decorated cave, such an unexpected and refreshing sight in this desert-like mountain range. With the newly researched link you can continue further on to connect with our Walk 20 to **Playa Blanca** (see the second extension) for an ultimate coastal discovery.

Access by car:
Drive to **Playa Quemada** to park near the entrance to the village. Then walk through the settlement to the cul-de-sac, **Calle Playa de la Arena**.

Access by bus: no service to **Playa Quemada**. Bus, or waterbus, to Puerto Calero then follow Walk2 to Playa Quemada (add 35mins 1.8kms).

Short Walks
a) To **Playa de la Arena** and return; 1 km, Ascents and descents 100 metres.
b) To **Playa del Pozo** and return; 4 km, Ascents and descents 220 metres.

Extensions
a) An ascent up to **Femés** from the dirt track joined at Wp.5, total of 7km, Ascents 550 metres (one way); see Walk 21.
b) A long coastal discovery to link with Walk 20 to **Playa Blanca**, total of 19km, Ascents and descents 700 metres (one way), vertigo risk (after Wp.10) and one short scramble (after Wp.13); see the end of the text.

From the western end of **Calle Playa de la Arena** (on the corner with **Calle Playa Mujeres**) (Wp.1 0M), a broad trail crosses the watercourse and climbs up onto the headland to a junction at a 'Monumento Natural Los Ajaches' pillar sign (Wp.2 3M), where the track to the right is our optional return route (from Wp.4), as we carry straight on to pass a cairn, after which the trail levels off. This whole region is criss-crossed by a mixture of

start of trail at Wp.1

trails which can cause confusion, so we recommend staying on the main trail.

Ahead, a clear trail zigzags up from the *barranco* behind **Playa de la Arena** as we start curving into the *barranco* to a zigzag descent. Taking care on the slippery surface, we drop down to a path junction (8M) where most people go left and down to the **Playa de la Arena** beach. We continue straight on, to climb the steep zigzag ascent onto the next headland, taking it one zig or zag at a time.

Our ascent brings us up to a T-junction (Wp.3 16M) whose right hand branch is traversing the slope. Going left, we immediately hit another junction where we bear right to reach another junction after 60 metres (Wp.4), where a second traversing path to the right is our alternative return route to avoid the descent and ascent through the *barranco*, connecting with Wp.2. Turning left, we are now traversing above the cliffs of a steep ridge, a popular *parapente* launch point, as we come along to cross a series of water runoffs of the side ravines.

Our route is very much into and out of *barrancos* interspersed with sea views, as we cross yet another small water runoff and stay on the best defined path out of this ravine from where our destination of **Playa del Pozo** comes into view. It might look close, but there are still a few obstacles in the way. Joining a dirt track (Wp.5 32M) coming from above, we follow it for 130 metres before a faint walking trail (Wp.6) forks off to our left. You can also use the dirt/stone track for the descent into **Barranco de la Higuera**.

Across from us on the opposite wall of the *barranco* we notice several eye-catching features: the refuge with the well, to the right of which is a ruined house backed by two signposted junctions (our continuation), but more interestingly an enormous stone art, a maritime anchor-style design. Taking the walking trail (Wp.6), we descend until the path peters out and we come onto a faint track (Wp.7) running along the ravine floor, 100 meters short of the coastline. Going left, we follow the track to the mouth of the *barranco*, where it swings right behind the boulder beach to bring us across to the refuge (Wp.8 62M) and *pozo* from which the beach takes its name. There is little, if any, shade at **Playa del Pozo** so make sure you are well protected against the sun.

signed junction at Wp.9

From the refuge (Wp.8 0M), we can cut across along a track (NW) to come directly to a signposted junction (Wp.9 3M) 30 metres above the ruin. Going uphill for 50 metres, we bear left at a Y-junction, our branch signed '**Peña de los Dises**'. Crossing a ravine's watercourse, we climb steadily, at one point very close to the edge of the steep escarpment, after which our path levels off for us to enjoy a pleasant section of the path traversing this plateau, a safe distance from the edge of the cliffs. Crossing several gullies, our path turns inland to cross a more substantial ravine's watercourse (Wp.10 15M) before swinging out of the *barranco*. We cross two more watercourses, the second dropping steeply into the ravine on our left, just before coming to a wayposted junction (Wp.11 19M) where a blue dot on a waypost indicates right up the broad *lomo*.

We go straight on and immediately swing right to stay on the main path, to have an unexpected view down into the ravine - it's a surprising sight given the isolation of these mountains - where by the beach we spot an immaculately maintained plant garden, locally known as *jardín secreto*, next to a cave full of surprises! The rock path takes us down to the valley floor to a broad riverbed of **Barranco de la Casita** (Wp.12 23M). Turning left, we go down the riverbed track to explore the **Secret Garden** next to the cave with a small shrine (Wp.13 25M). In the cave there is an abundance of artefacts and gifts from the ocean; a great spot to take a break before continuing or returning.

Wp.13, cave of surprises

Our return is a retracing of our outward route until we reach the junction at Wp.4 where we keep straight on instead of dropping into the *barranco*. Our path runs inland, and as is the way of this area, a second path parallels our route twenty metres lower down the *barranco*, gently descending slopes covered with goat traces. We are heading towards a junction of barren valleys that con-join inland of **Playa de la Arena**. At a faint junction a trace goes ahead while our path turns right, its continuation is clearly seen across the valley, for us to join the second (lower) path at the gravel-lined watercourse. Now we have a steady ascent up the grit-surfaced path, easier to ascend than descend, to come onto a faint track which runs along the *lomo*. We head back down the track towards the sea to rejoin our outward route.

Extension - a link to Walk 20 and Walk 9 to **Playa Blanca**

Refreshed by the enlivening sight in these otherwise barren mountains, we return from the **Secret Garden** onto the main path (Wp.12 0M) and climb steeply out of the ravine before traversing the vertiginous sharp escarpment above the *jardín*. After crossing a 'rockfall' watercourse, our path goes steeply up a rough boulder-strewn gully with black lava surface before it swings left, out of the gully (Wp.14 7M) by a pair of cairns (or 20 metres before the black surface turns into brown if you came that far - easy to overlook!).

Our path now levels off and soon turns inland to cross a ravine's watercourse after which we climb gently to come to a vantage point (Wp.15 13M) overlooking a long beach; it seems that our path almost plunges down from here. On our skittery descent we have one obstacle we need to negotiate carefully - a 'rock step' that we scramble down slowly, before the gradient eases for us to come down to the beach.

bunker before Wp.16

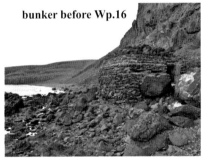

We follow the pebbly beach, shadowing a faint track which runs out before passing a bunker under the cliffs, big boulders slowing down our progress. Back on pebbles after the bunker, we are back to a brisk pace to come almost to the end of the beach, where we find a mouth of a ravine with a track going inland (Wp.16 28M).

Taking the dirt track (W), we now need to employ a sense of orientation as we are facing a more difficult navigation part of our route. When the *barranco* widens and the slopes on our left become less steep, we note a pair of beige-coloured gullies running parallel, resembling a jeep track going straight down. 220 metres after leaving the beach, still before the 'jeep track' gullies, we bear left (Wp.17 31M) on a very faint path, looking for cairns. The path climbs towards these gullies before crossing them to continue on their right side. The cairn-marked path eventually turns slightly right and away from the gullies to emerge on a dirt track (Wp.18 39M) on a ridge, which, whether or not you stick exactly to the path, is in any case hard to miss as it extends along the whole length of the ridge line.

Turning right (W), we climb along the track for 100 metres to reach a major dirt track (Wp.19 42M) where we join Walk 20, which continues south-east. From here on we follow Walk 20 to reach **Playa Blanca**.

The most difficult thing about this walk is getting a place on the walk itself. This is one of the two official guided walks in the **Timanfaya** and you need to book a slot (free of charge) at www.reservasparquesnacionales.es where you can pick the guided walk in English or Spanish. Once confirmed, you'll get an email with a reservation code and all necessary details.

Numbers are limited to one or two (depending on the day) mini buses, each carrying eight walkers and at the time of preparing this edition, the walks in English go on Monday, Tuesday, Wednesday and Friday. This is the general rule, however depending on availability of the guides the days might occasionally differ. Given the increasing popularity of this guided walk, it is getting even more difficult to secure a place so we recommend booking well before you leave for Lanzarote. The booking is possible max 2 months ahead. It is essential to speak the language the guided walk is offered in and have proper closed footwear as per the instructions. We have witnessed tourists who recklessly arrived to the meeting point in sandals and were disallowed by the ranger to join the group. Not that the terrain is difficult, but once on the route, it's the rangers who have responsibility for the group and its progress, so they will care about the shoes you're wearing. Don't forget to bring your ID along with the booking number.

Access by car: Depending on the day of the week, the meeting points are either the **Visitor's Centre** or downtown **Yaiza**. **Centro de Visitantes** is on the LZ-67 road between **Yaiza** and **Mancha Blanca**. If approaching from south, drive past the entrance to **Timanfaya National Park**, and the **Visitors' Centre** is the next major building on your left, 4 kilometres further along the road. Make sure you arrive on time - rangers do not wait for latecomers.

Access by bus: Not suitable for bus access.

Assuming you've managed the rather difficult task of securing a place, then at the agreed hour it's all aboard the minibus, followed by a chilled drive to the trailhead.

Most of the days there are two groups coming against each other, rangers swapping their car keys as they meet about half-way into the walk. If there's just one group, the profile of the route changes to a circuit of about the same distance as the linear route.

ranger giving an explanation

Depending on the group, you'll either have a bit of uphill or downhill during your route, but this is hardly noticeable due to the slow nature of the walking lecture tour. It's an interesting tour amongst almost virgin lava,

short lava education session

with examples of volcanic tubes or *jameos*, including one you can stand in, and you'll learn about the different types of lava: the *lapilli*, or fine ash, the *malpaís* or *'AA' scoria* lava which is sharp and jagged, the pahoehoe type that has set in smooth swags, and lava bombs.

The guides park the buses at each end of the manicured track and off we go, frequently pausing for a short lecture. They are well versed in the facts and myths of the **Timanfaya** as we amble through the unique landscape on this strolling lecture tour.

For everyone interested in the historical and volcanic background of the **Timanfaya**, this is a 'Must Do' tour, though you will have to sift the fact from myth; for example, if "…a footstep takes three years to disappear ...." then why is there no sign of the workers' footmarks who created this manicured track? Nevertheless, you will learn a lot about the exciting yet terrifying 1730s, the time when nobody really knew if, and when, the eruptions would come to an end, about what followed and how it affected local people's lives.

This is a guided-only walk, meaning it is prohibited to do individually, so trying it solo is risking the attention of Lanzarote's 'lava police'. If you prefer to be on your own in **Timanfaya**, look at our 'El Golfo Circular' route, which is the second of the two guided walks offered by the *parque nacional*. Unlike **Termesana**, you can undertake that one individually.

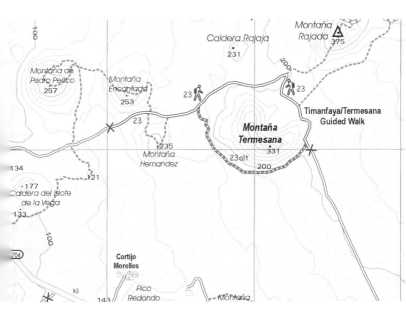

This is a second of the two guided walks at **Timanfaya National Park**, but unlike **Termesana** you can do this route on your own without booking. The authorities have picked this route for a reason: along the route, which follows well established tracks or trails, we enjoy contrasts of green tabaiba-dotted *islotes* surrounded by new flows of jagged lava. Spectacular in its own right, it is more variable than **Termesana** as it also includes a coastal section with a beach break for a short picnic (should you do the guided version). The return coastal route is not recommended when the sea is extremely rough.

If you don't mind being part of a group up to 10 people we recommend doing the guided version of the walk, provided you have luck securing a spot - not an easy task as the guided walks are getting increasingly popular; see '23 Termesana Guided Walk' for booking details. The 'official' route is the same as our route including the 1km diversion to **Playa del Paso**.

* 3 ½ to 4 hours if guided (including breaks and picnic)   ** in **El Golfo**

Access by car: take the LZ-703 or LZ-704 to **El Golfo** and drive through the settlement to the car park at the end of tarmac by the playground.

Access by bus: no bus connection.

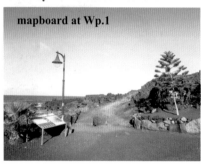

mapboard at Wp.1

From the mapboard at the north-western corner of the parking (Wp.1 0M), where we study the route's profile, we walk 70 metres south-east to find a trail (Wp.2 1M) heading inland (E) amongst groves of tabaiba dulce. All the fauna and flora are very well adapted here and the plants drop their leaves during the highest temperatures due to scarcity of water, but if you are here outside of the summer temperatures, you are likely to walk through a lush green land. We keep heading east, our trail widening to a track, and note a new lava flow in a very distinct form not far on our right, surrounding an older strip of land that we walk on - an *islote* (isle), where fauna and flora has already developed.

We come to a junction with a substantial dirt track (Wp.3 15M) in sight of white houses. Turning left, we follow the smooth track past the farmhouses (Wp.4 18M), with examples of plots covered by fine lava ashes behind their stone wall. The ash is known as the *lapilli* lava or *picón*, commonly used in Lanzarote's farming as the top-most layer to reduce water evaporation. Our track winds along and climbs very gently to join the edge of the new lava flow, quite spectacular to observe the contrast formed by its jagged rocks on the right and the easy-on-the-eye farmlands on our left. Passing four tracks off

Wp.5 gateposts

left to the farms, we come to a T-junction of tracks with tall concrete gate posts (Wp.5 31M).

Bearing left between the posts, we skirt the base of **Montaña Quemada**, an older cone covered by ashes of a newer eruption, flanks of the mountain dotted by *zocos* protecting fig trees. Once a vital source of nutrition along with cereals, the fig trees are nowadays left neglected or are maintained only as a hobby. On our left we pass a ruined house with a good example of an *aljibe*, the underground water tank being a reminder of difficult times way before the construction of desalination plants.

We come to pass beneath a large villa (Wp.6 41M), after which our track swings north-west to pass a statue of the Timanfaya devil. The land on both sides is dominated by traces of old stone walls, nature gradually reclaiming it, as we walk into the national park past a boundary sign, before coming to a vehicle barrier (Wp.7 46M) on the edge of a new lava flow. The 'Prohibido el paso' sign applies only to vehicles, not walkers.

Timanfaya devil

Behind the barrier we are amidst a new lava flow, passing an access track to a hut off to the right to briefly come onto a plant-dotted *islote*, ignoring a left fork, before returning onto the sinister looking flow of the dark new lava. **Montaña Halcones** on our right

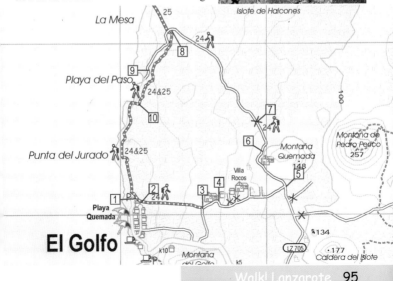

with its tabaiba-strewn slopes is an excellent example of an *islote* surrounded by a maw of the new lava; its name Halcones referring to falcons nesting there.

Our track takes us to a crossroads (Wp.8 68M) with the coastal trail at a mapboard, where the left branch across the rough grit is our return way back to **El Golfo**. We take the chance to visit **Playa del Paso** beach, keeping straight ahead to descend along the track below a lava wall to the beach (Wp.9 75M).

After the beach break (0M), we climb back to the crossroads (Wp.8 8M) and take the gritty trail (S), which immediately enters an older lava flow where plants are slowly colonising the area. There are no branches until **El Golfo** and the trail is well trodden, but the surface is tricky, requiring careful footwork; sections of polished stones and sand alternate with sharp lava. We pass a small rock arch on our right with views down to **Playa del Paso** before crossing a partly collapsed lava tube; its obvious fragility reminds us how unwise it would be to leave the trail in a land full of such lava tunnels. After a smoother section we pass the national park limits sign (Wp.10 37M), just after which our trail very briefly turns west, bringing the beach along with cliffs into view. It is up and down the rough lava path, which runs near the cliffs as we

chilling amidst the lava

catch first glimpses of white houses of **El Golfo**, appearing as if rising from the dark badlands. Our trail eventually broadens and becomes sandy before coming down to the car park by the playground (60M).

Our third **Timanfaya** route has a surreal nature all of its own for most of the route, as we walk along a coastal path between the Atlantic Ocean on our right and the 'Lava Sea' on our left. It is long and linear so best suited to our 2CSK approach or walking groups with minibus support.

We start at the achingly lovely **Playa de la Madera**, and eleven kilometres later join our **El Golfo Circular** to finish in the seaside settlement. Good hiking footwear is essential for this rocky lava trail if you are to avoid bruising the soles of your feet.

Access by car:
From **Tinajo** take the minor road towards **Tenezar** coastal settlement. When the road turns sharp right, continue straight ahead on a wide dirt road. Ignore all side turnings, and as the surface changes to *picón* look for somewhere to park; note this is six kms of bumpy dirt road from when you leave the tarmac. On no account try to drive down to the beach area at **Playa de la Madera**.

From your parking place, walk down the track onto **Playa de la Madera** (Wp.1 0M), a wonderfully isolated black beach with the Atlantic waves crashing onto the edge of the 'Lava Sea', and climb up the path onto the lava sea.

This is a wonderful setting, with the ocean crashing against the lava and small lava points on our right, while on our left the 'lava sea' rolls away to the distant **Timanfaya** fire mountains. Amongst the lava sea are points of higher ground around which the slow moving lava flowed, known locally as *islotes*; these green islands harbour local flora which stand out in sharp contrast against the barren lava.

Playa de la Madera

Caletón Estrecho

29

1

Paletón

Punta del Paletón

22

Islote de los Betancores

Piedra Corujo 25

Bajito Blanco

Punta del Roncador

Tinajo
Yaiza

100

So it's onward, one step after another along the rocky path, stopping occasionally to take in the views, which all seem remarkably like the views you stopped for earlier. It is a strange combination of beauty and monotony.

We have 9.5 kilometres before **Montaña Halcones** rises out of the jagged sea on our left, indicating that we will soon be briefly leaving the coast. Our path finally turns away from the ocean and winds along (SSE) to meet a dirt track (Wp.2 200M).

Across the dirt track we take our **El Golfo** route (see Walk 24) taking care to stay on the official trail all the way along to the beach car park by the playground (Wp.3 250M).

We could just jump into our waiting vehicle but after all that beautiful isolation it would be a waste not to reacquaint ourselves with humanity in the form of refreshments in **El Golfo**'s choice of cafes and restaurants.

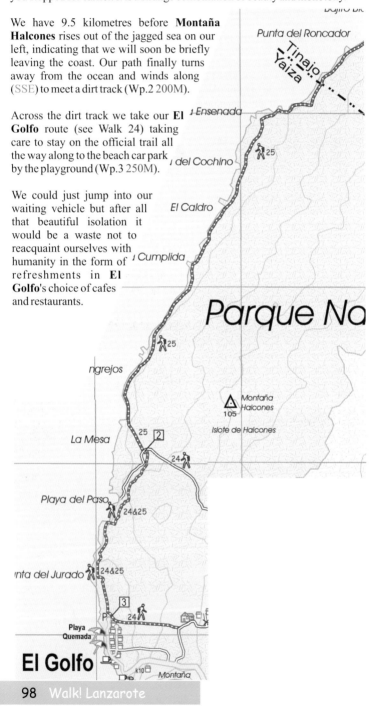

Montaña Cuervo is a true gem, so much so that if you miss this little route you will miss much of what Lanzarote has to offer. Vulcanologists will marvel at the condition of the exploded volcanic cone, while the rest of us simply stare in awe at the truly spectacular *caldera*.

Since the last edition of Walk! Lanzarote the car parks and access trail have been completed, slightly changing our start.

Access by car: Our start is at the large picon car park at Km4.3 of the LZ-56.

Access by bus: no bus connection.

Short Walk

This walk is already short, but if you are only interested in the truly spectacular, then go into the caldera and return.

We leave the car park at the LZ-56 on a boulderlined track (Wp.1 0M) to head (SSW) towards the small mountain. **Montaña Cuervo** is not a big mountain, but rising up out of the lava sea, its sharp image contrasts with the fuzzy lava, lending it a mystical presence even from this distance.

approaching Montaña Cuervo

An easy stroll along the cinder track takes us past a track off to our left, to swing left and then right amidst the sea of lava to come to the base of the cone (Wp.2 14M) where we enter the

circular leg of our route (N). We shun the steep *picón* path climbing to the lip of the crater (prohibited) and follow our track around the cone (NNW), a lava 'wave' cutting out the views as we pass another steep *picón* path ascending the crater shortly before coming to a surprise (Wp.3 18M); the huge gash in the side of the volcanic cone which gives access to its interior.

inside the crater Wp.4

To descend the path beneath huge volcanic boulders into the *caldera* is to enter another world. From the road, you'd never guess that this stunning interior landscape of a volcano was awaiting you. From our viewpoint on the floor of the crater (Wp.4), the geology is simply awesome, while at the western end of the crater, 110 metres away (Wp.5), wild pink geraniums colonise the floor and slopes, adding to the unreality of this surreal experience.

People spend hours in this crater where time has little meaning, so when you choose to depart we'll restart our timing at the crater entrance (Wp.3 0M) as we head west around the cone on a *picón* track running between the mountain and the lava 'wave' on our right. The wave is broken by a track (Wp.6) which heads towards **Timanfaya**, the break giving us a chance to look out over this great 'lava sea'.

As we circle the extended cone, we pass another track going out into lava fields (Wp.7 8M) and admire more colonies of wild geraniums blooming in the most unforgiving landscape you could imagine, particularly numerous in one floriferous area seemingly at odds with the surroundings, which also sustains Vinagrera (Rumex lunaria), Lanzarote Firebush or Aulaga (Launaea arborescens), and Nicotiana glauca.

Our track runs gently downhill past a track heading out into the lava (Wp.8) and curves around the mountain (SSE) as we come into view of volcanoes in the winemaking region of **La Geria**, then passing a series of lava ledges (Wp.9 16M) on our right, clearly indicating the thin, harder surfaced crusts above a softer core that you'll be warned not to step on if you take the **Timanfaya** guided walk. We crunch along the *picón* track curving (ENE) towards the main bulk of the mountain rising above cinder dunes, the dunes and cinder slopes being briefly replaced by bedrock (Wp.10) shortly before we come back to our outward route (26M). Arriving back at our car, we can only marvel at this 'gem' of an easy walking route, almost literally in the middle of nowhere.

approaching our outward route

A short drive (N) from **Montaña Cuervo** we arrive in the large palm-dotted parking area at the top of the LZ-56 for our adventure on **Montaña Los Rodeos**. This a route of such comforting simplicity with good conditions underfoot that it could be regarded as a stroll suitable for all the family. Simple yet interesting, as while we get right up close to the pristine lava fields, literally 'nose to nose', we do so on an easy walking surface. We didn't climb to the peak - that wind again - but if it's calm you have the option of a hundred metre ascent/descent on a rough jeep track to take in the stunning views from the summit.

Access by car: Park in the large palm-studded parking area on the west of the LZ-56 at km0.4. Note that this is out in the country, so don't leave anything in your car while you are walking.

At the top of the parking area a tarmac lane heads NW accessing the farmed plots as it heads out to meet the LZ-67 just south of our access to Walk 28.

Access by bus: no bus connection.

We start at the junction where a dirt track heads SW off the lane (Wp.1 0M) to walk down the dirt track with **Montaña Cortijo** rising on our right in contrast to the lava plain on our left as we pass a cave/hut cut into the base of the small mountain (Wp.2 6M).

As dirt tracks go this is an immaculate top of the range example whose firm even surface makes for easy walking taking us to a junction (Wp.3 13M) where a minor track services a cultivated *picón* plot set below **Montañas Rostros** and **Cortijo**. We stay on the main track which now swings towards the south taking us directly towards **Los Rodeos**. Steadily, **Los Rodeos** dominates our view ahead until it is looming above us when we come to a T-junction (Wp.4 23M) directly facing the peak.

Starting out

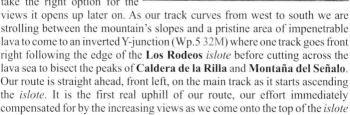

You could go either left (clockwise) or right (anticlockwise) around **Los Rodeos** but our choice is to take the right option for the views it opens up later on. As our track curves from west to south we are strolling between the mountain's slopes and a pristine area of impenetrable lava to come to an inverted Y-junction (Wp.5 32M) where one track goes front right following the edge of the **Los Rodeos** *islote* before cutting across the lava sea to bisect the peaks of **Caldera de la Rilla** and **Montaña del Señalo**. Our route is straight ahead, front left, on the main track as it starts ascending the *islote*. It is the first real uphill of our route, our effort immediately compensated for by the increasing views as we come onto the top of the *islote*

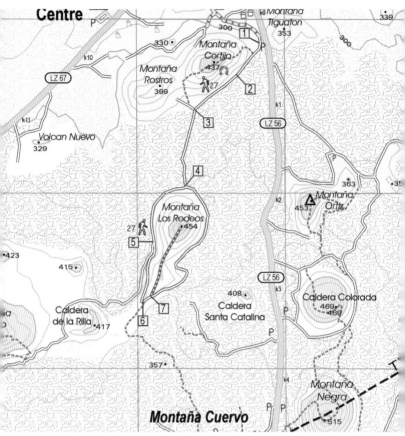

(Wp.6 42M).

So far our views have been limited, this being a flat route, so looking up at the peaks and out over the western lava as we climb onto the *islote*, now we have the eastern views. Should you think these are more of the same, lava fields dotted with volcanic cones, then look down below. Along the eastern side of the **Los Rodeos** *islote* is a green lava river, frozen where it set but its rippled surface giving the appearance of movement - it is for this view that we went right at the T-junction.

Our track continues running down the eastern side of the *islote* where eighty metres on we come to the rough jeep track (Wp.7 44M) that ascends 'straight up' to the summit of **Los Rodeos**; an ascent of just over a hundred metres giving us an energetic option to extend our route so long as the wind is not blowing. A gentle descent brings us down to the level of the lava while our track snakes around the base of the *islote* to bring us back to the T-junction (Wp.4 54M). Here we turn right to stroll back along the smooth track to the parking area (Wp.1 77M).

This in our personal opinion is a 'top 3' walk on Lanzarote, if not the single best, which includes experiencing the 'lava sea' followed by climbing the crater rim of the *caldera* along with a surprising sight to go with superb views from the rim. There are no refreshments (a short drive away) but then, no route is completely perfect!

This is one of the new routes encouraged by the island government, who have opened up and improved the path through the lava sea to reach the **Caldereta** and **Caldera Blanca** craters. Previously you could only approach them from the north after a lengthy off-tarmac drive which would negate your hire car insurance.

Walking along the crater rim, we overlook very steep slopes down to the floor of the *caldera* which might upset vertigo sufferers. That said, the ridge is broad and the path never really exposed. Only undertake this route in good weather conditions - dry and with low windspeeds.

Access by car:
To get to the start, take the dirt track off the LZ-67 just west of **Mancha Blanca** from a junction signposted 'El Tablero' (70 metres W of Km8); there is a route signboard at this junction. Take the easily driveable dirt track signed 'Montaña Caldereta' to its end at a small parking area for a dozen cars. If the parking area is full, go back to **Mancha Blanca**, park and walk in; don't park on the dirt track as it is in regular use by farmers.

Access by bus: the nearest bus stop is in **Mancha Blanca**, line 16 (**Arrecife/La Santa**), adding an extra 1.7km (one way) to walk to the start.

From the end of the car park (Wp.1 0M) we continue on the *picón* track (W), which in a few metres peters out for us to come onto the new trail of crunching grit cut through the lava field. While the trail is well made, just look each side to see what conditions would be like without it. It is stony underfoot giving us a rocking gait as we slowly progress towards the northern rim of **Caldereta** which shields the bulk of **Caldera Blanca** from this viewpoint.

Any thoughts that this is a calm lava sea are dispelled as we drop into a valley formed between waves of lava - it's quite surreal to think that this was molten magma that set into the shapes we now see. After winding across the floor our trail climbs out of the valley into a seriously disrupted landscape of peaks and holes like an angry sea frozen in rock formations. Our trail guides us through this wild barren landscape to a junction (Wp.2 18M), the path to our right having stones across it. Keeping to the main trail, we snake our way through the lava, passing a small tree growing in the centre of the trail, unusual in this barren waste. As we curve around the north of **Caldereta** we leave the lava sea (Wp.3 25M) for the luxury of a dirt path and flower-bedecked slopes (in February) as we come up to a junction at a clump of trees by the entrance to **Caldereta** (Wp.4 31M).

This marks the start of the circular part of our tour, our return route coming in along the right branch across the lava, as we turn left towards the mouth of **Caldereta**. Just a few steps off the main trail alongside a stone wall brings us below a ruined hut to the view into the *caldera*. What looked like a small cone

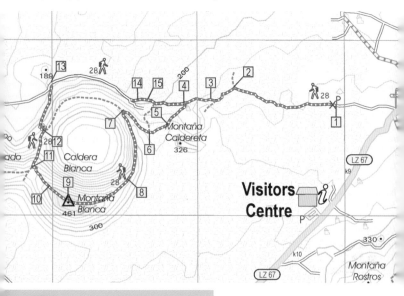

climbing Caldereta slopes after Wp.4

compared to **Caldera Blanca** is a most impressive sight. From the entrance there's a tempting option to follow a steep path ascending to the *caldera*'s rim. Back on the main trail, we climb steadily along the outer slopes o f **C a l d e r e t a** u n t i l, approximately half way up the cone, our trail turns to cross the lava (Wp.5). If the previous lava was an angry sea, then this is a furious torrent of tortured rock trapped between two volcanic cones; after the manicured paths so far we're now on bare rock, following cairns for our route across the torrent. If in doubt about the route then scan ahead for the next cairn before heading off.

After twisting, turning and clambering from cairn to cairn across the lava we come onto a dirt path (Wp.6 42M) and a junction where we go right so that in forty metres we bear left to angle up towards the **Caldera Blanca** rim (the path straight ahead alongside the mountain base continues past corrals to prematurely meet our return route at Wp.15, but it would be a crime to skip the best of the route!). A traverse across the slope on the faint worn path, including going through a rock 'channel', brings us up onto a low point of the crater rim (Wp.7 52M) to find that it consists of a broad top up to five metres wide, before it rolls off to near vertical slopes dropping to the *caldera* floor.

Surprisingly, the floor of the *caldera* way below us is covered in abundant vegetation, a direct contrast to the landscape outside the volcanic cone. What we first take to be dots resolves into a large flock of goats apparently enjoying the rich grazing found in this verdant and unlikely oasis.

Buoyed by the views, we set off up the great curving slope of the rim towards the summit, the views expanding over the southern lava fields as we climb while to the north over the crater rim we look out over the lava and **Montaña Teneza** to the Atlantic Ocean.

The first third of the ascent is easy uphill walking until we come to wind-sculpted rock ledges providing amphitheatre style seating where we take a break (Wp.8 72M). Now the climbing becomes more seríous as we climb from ledge to ledge before the final ascent on the narrowing rim to the summit cairn and trig point (Wp.9 86M 461m). The views have to be seen to be believed - the goats really are dots down on the *caldera* floor, while looking down the southern face we find

approaching the summit, Caldereta on right

that Lanzarote's outdoor artists have been at work creating giant footprints and a huge mouse/rat from lava rocks at the base of the mountain. From the summit the only way is down as we carefully pick our way around the western rim to come down onto a goat trail whose loose surface needs careful concentration before a path finally emerges (Wp.10 92M) to take us down to a crossroads of paths at the saddle (Wp.11 100M) between **Caldera Blanca** and **Risco Quebrado**. Bearing right (NE), our path takes us back onto the *caldera* rim.

Down below it is surprising to see so many cultivated fields on the *islotes* set amongst the lava sea. Our path follows the rim until its lowest point where we start our zigzag descent (Wp.12 110M) down the western slope on the remains of a stone-laid donkey trail. At the end of the zigzags we are onto a 'normal' dirt walking trail interspersed with tricky rock sections running down before bearing right onto a path just above an old *picón* plot to meet with a dirt track (Wp.13 124M). Now we are into relaxed walking round the northern base of the *caldera*, our track clenched between the base of the cone and a new lava flow as we head through a welcoming green section of grass and trees to cross a stream at an eroded section, where we turn away from the mountain. The track runs out by a 'Montaña Caldereta' signpost for us to pick up the trail across the lava (Wp.14 140M) below some *corrals*. Now it is back onto a rocking gait before a lava path from the *corrals* joins us from our right (Wp.15 142M). Passing a right fork to a small grassy clearing with agave, we come to the far side of the lava 'torrent' where we meet up with our outward trail (Wp.4).

We retrace our outward route back through the lava 'angry sea' landscape to the parking area by which time, after that bobbly rocking gait finish, we're glad to be thinking of finding some suitable refreshments to celebrate a compact and spectacular route..

The unique agricultural landscape of **La Geria** is one of Lanzarote's most photographed features. At close quarters the 'grape pits' do not look that impressive, but add a bit of altitude and how that perspective changes into an amazing landscape.

A linear walk from **Uga** to **Puerto del Carmen**, with options for **Montaña Tinasoria** (easy) and the ascent of **Montaña de Guardilama** (tough and not on windy days) for its awesome views. No refreshments en-route, but there are bars in **Uga** with **Bar/Rest Gregorío** near our start.

*Timings in the walk are for the linear route direct to **Puerto del Carmen**. For the excursion to **Montaña Tinasoria** add 1 hour, 2km and 150 metres of ascents/descents, for the ascent of **Guardilama** add 1.5 hours, 2.5km and 350 metres of ascents/descents.

Access by bus:
The Nº60(**Arrecife/Playa Blanca**) bus calls at **Uga**.

We start from the bus stop by **Uga** church (Wp.1 0M) to walk (SE) down to the end of **Calle Jorge Rodriguez**. Going straight ahead, past cul-de-sacs left and right, we come up to a junction (Wp.2) where we go left on **Calle Los Arenales**, a narrow road heading NE above a small park. After a house on our right, we take a dirt road to the right (Wp.3) which climbs steeply up to the **Teguise** road; alongside the track are our first examples of **La Geria** 'grape pits'. On the narrow main road, we head away from **Uga** (NW) to take the first dirt road off to the right (Wp.4 17M). Now we're into the **La Geria** grape growing area proper, though in these early stages there are more fields and terraces than the traditional grape vine *zocos* (depressions of volcanic ash enclosed in a horseshoe-shaped wall of volcanic rock with a vine planted in its centre). As we progress, the track runs along a plateau above **La Geria** for us

to look across a landscape of *zocos* backed by the volcanic peaks of the **Timanfaya**.

Turning off the tarmac at Wp.4

Figs alternate with grapes as we climb steadily past a track off to the right (Wp.5), the **La Geria** landscape expanding into thousands of horseshoe-shaped depressions covering the whole region as we pass a second chained track on our right (Wp.6). Away on our left is one of the large *bodegas* as we continue uphill past the *bodega* access track (Wp.7) towards the pass. A steady ascent takes us over a junction (Wp.8) and brings us up onto the pass (Wp.9 57M) from where we can take a break for the views over the unique **La Geria** landscape. Now, if you think these views are impressive, think what another 100 or 200 metres altitude would do.

Tinasoria Option

Just past the top of the pass we take a track (Wp.10 0M) on our right to walk steadily uphill (SW), keeping right at a junction (Wp.11 3M); a popular 'jumping off' point for hang-gliders. Our track brings us up to an abandoned farm (Wp.12 10M) with an interesting collection of water cisterns. Beyond the farm the track deteriorates, splits, rejoins, and then dwindles to trail width as we curve towards the west in a steady ascent giving us expanding views over the south of the island as we come up to the trig point (Wp.13 24M). Beyond the trig point is a rough natural stone bench for seating while we take in the panorama south and west of us.

The water cisterns

Guardilama Option

If you are feeling fit and it's a calm day, then how about climbing **Guardilama** for the unforgettable views from its summit? Only attempt this on the calmest days as the wind sheer makes this route potentially dangerous. Not recommended for vertigo sufferers.

We go over the pass and in a few metres take a track to the left (Wp.14) to walk up past grapes enclosed by stone walls. After the last of the stone walls the track continues straight up the mountain. This truly is a 'puff and grunt' ascent, taking frequent breaks to get our breath back. The track peters out half way up, after which we follow a faint trail straight up over the open ground; another 50 metres of ascent and a few more stops for breath sees us reach the summit (Wp.15). The views are simply awesome. **Guardilama** is Lanzarote's most 'pointy' accessible peak. The **La Geria** plain lies some 300

La Geria and Montaña Guardilama

metres below us, and the views over the volcanic cones of the **Timanfaya** are unforgettable.

Stay as long as your vertigo will allow to enjoy the island's most spectacular views. Take care on the steep descent, watching every step you make; it is all too easy to be distracted by the views and lose your footing on the steep ground.

Onward to Puerto del Carmen

From the pass we follow the dirt road down into the more familiar Lanzarote landscape, a steady descent bringing us down to a T-junction (Wp.16). Here we leave the **GR131** continuing on **Camino del Mesón** as we turn right to

head downhill past a clutch of houses. We stay on the main track, passing a nice house and track on our left. The track becoming tarmacked as we head down to cross the **Asomada** road (Wp.17 77M). Straight over the road, and we're back on the **Camino del Mesón** to come down past **Villa Vistas** to a crossroads of tracks (Wp.18) to continue straight over and come down to a junction (Wp.19). Going right (S) we stroll down to the end of **Camino Los Olivos** to go left on a narrow lane, then right onto a track to carefully cross the fast and busy LZ-2 main road (Wp.20).

We're back on a dusty track running (SSE) down through the general wasteland that lies between mountains and sea, a wasteland dotted with 'exclusively desirable villa residences' in estate agent speak. At the end of **Camino La Calderina** (Wp.21 97M) we take the track to the right (S), keeping left at the next junction (Wp.22) to pass **Finca Lomos Altos** before reaching a T-junction; here we go right to come onto the end of a tarmac lane (Wp.23) at another T-junction. Going left (E) passing a lane off to the left then one to the right, we come to a lane off left to the main road. Keeping to our tarmac lane, we come to a second lane (Wp.24 120M) linking us to the **Puerto del Carmen** road.

If at this stage you are growing tired of the bungalow-dotted wilderness you could take to the main road for an easy tarmac stroll down to the *circunvalación* roundabout, followed by pavements down into the resort.

Those of us choosing to stick with the grit head down (S) **Camino Barranco de Quiquere** past the multi-tiered garden of **Casa la Helice** for an easy stroll down past the grandly named little track of **Camino las Casanas** before coming onto the **Puerto Calero** road (Wp.25 138M). Straight over the road, we continue on the track down to the mouth of the *barranco* where we meet the route of Walk 2 (Wp.26). From here we follow the coastal promenade (E) back to the 'old town' of **Puerto del Carmen** (172M).

Not everyone desires a long linear walking route that finishes in Lanzarote's main resort. More than a few walkers using hire cars for their exploration ask us for circular routes, preferably with safe car parking and good refreshments. If this is you, then here's your route as we take the classic **La Geria** and convert it into a circular, based on the laid-back town of **Uga**. Our additions include one kilometre of road walking but the majority is on tracks we've not previously covered.

4   2½ H   11 km   490m / 490m   ↻   3*

*at start and end

Access by car:
From the LZ-2 exit at the **Uga/Femés** roundabout onto the LZ-30 then take the first street left, to park at the edge of the town - or continue into **Uga** for onstreet parking near the church.

Access by bus: Bus N°60 between **Arrecife** and **Playa Blanca** leaves from both destinations on the hour and calls at **Uga** church, Mon-Fri with a reduced service on Sat/Sun/fiestas.

We follow the classic **La Geria** route until it crosses the **La Asomada** road (Wps.1-8 77M); see Walk 29 for detailed description. Note we have condensed the detailed waypoints of Walk 29 1 to17 to the main junctions of the **La Geria** classic route.

Instead of crossing the road, we turn right to walk down the road towards the roundabout on the LZ-2. We pass two lanes on our right until, just before the roundabout (Wp.9 87M), we come to a dirt track on our right which has been 'rocked off' to prevent vehicle access.

Leaving the tarmac we step through the boulders to follow the dirt track (W) to a junction with a more substantial dirt track (Wp.10 91M) which runs out to the LZ-2 on our left. Going right, we follow the track gently uphill to an isolated house, **Casa Cañada** (Wp.11 98M), passing it on our left to continue uphill along the track.

We pass a track on our left, which accesses a cultivated plot alongside the LZ-2, before arriving at a crossroads of tracks (Wp.12 107M). We're overlooking **Caballo Lanzarote** (SW) with views south to **Playa Quemada** and **Puerto Calero**, the sixty metres we've ascended since Wp.9 already providing us with expanded views across the southern coastal plain. From the crossroads we go right (N) for the steady ascent up the track under the shadow of **Montaña Tinasoria**. It's a steady hundred metre ascent, never steep enough to be called serious but uphill all the way for the next kilometre; if you'd like an easier return, then the track straight across the junction (W) runs across above **Caballo Lanzarote** to join the LZ-30 with only thirty metres of ascents; however, we've not walked that route.

Pointing our noses north, we head up the track across the sloping plain below **Tinasoria** to pass under the high tension power lines with their red and white poles (Wp.13 109M). **Tinasoria** looms large above us as we gradually ascend to the ridge line to find ourselves overlooking the edge of the *zocos* area (Wp.14 122M). The *zocos* in this section are of relatively recent construction, their neat appearance a contrast with the older *zocos* on the earlier section of our route; as a viewpoint over **La Geria** this is one of the best. With the ascent behind us, we follow the track along the southern side of the ridge formed by **Montaña Norte** to a goat farm on the north of the track where we get more northern views (Wp.15 130M). From here it's steadily downhill passing a faint track off to our left bisecting **Montañas Majada** and **Mojón**, followed by a strange concrete structure (a water chute?) on our left (Wp.16 136M) before our track becomes a street, lined by houses on its southern side, which takes us down to the LZ-30 at the entrance to **Casa El Morro** (Wp.17 142M).

The water chute

Carefully across the main road we walk down the street (our car access) to meet our outward route at the open area crossroads where continuing straight on brings us to our starting point beside the church square and a choice of bar/restaurants for refreshment (148M).

31 Montaña Sóo Circuit

The circuit of **Montaña Sóo** is a real surprise - the charm of this route is that it provides a great adventure where you don't really expect it. Just after leaving the outskirts of **Sóo**, we are immediately rewarded by expanding views towards **Famara**. Circling the mountain, we come to a sand surprise before climbing to get more views: **Isla Graciosa** and **Alegranza**, a charming hidden crater and plains of **La Santa** all make this route incredibly panoramic and a true stunner.

Access by car: Park in **Sóo** at **Centro Socio Cultural 'El Buen Lugar'**, 80 metres west of the **Tiagua** turn-off.

Access by bus: Line 20 runs between **Arrecife** and **Caleta de Famara**, line 33 between **Tiagua** and **Costa Teguise**. Alight at the **Tiagua** turn-off and follow the main road (W) through the village to reach the start.

Short version: a circuit of **Pico Colorado** makes an impressive short route. We bear sharp left at Wp.5 to climb alongside the gully. The swift climb brings us to a carved gateway from which an unexpectedly beautiful sight of a little valley opens up. From the vantage point, we overlook a substantial part of the valley where a path, then dirt track run through the quiet *caldera* to link with the main route at Wp.12, where we bear left to take the traversing path (3.5kms, Ascents and descents 80 metres).

Centro Cultural at Wp.1

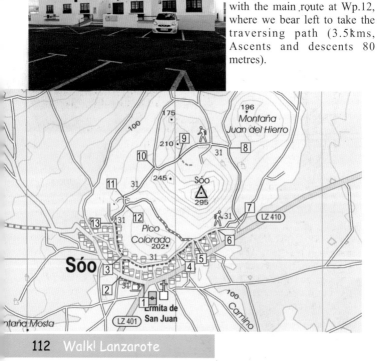

view of the isles from approaching Wp.9

From the **Centro Socio Cultural 'El Buen Lugar'** (Wp.1 0M), we follow the pavement along the village road (W), passing **Bar Coscofe** and a minimarket, before bearing right into **Calle Sargento Rojas** (Wp.2 3M) just before palms begin to line the main road. A steady climb brings us to a Y-junction (Wp.3 6M) with our return route coming in from the left, as we turn right to stroll along the tarmac street. Houses gradually give up as we pass a nice villa on our left, followed by a tarmac lane off to our right (Wp.4 16M), 100 metres after which we pass a dilapidated house on the left.

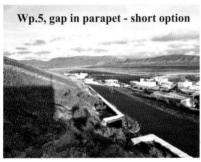

Wp.5, gap in parapet - short option

60 metres past the decrepit house, we come to a gap in the parapet (Wp.5 19M) - here the short option via the crater of **Pico Colorado** diverges from the main route. If you opt for the main route, we do recommend the 100-metre diversion to the left. A brisk climb brings you to the 'gateway' - well worth the look into the quiet *caldera*!

Our main route keeps following the tarmac as we enjoy consistently good views to **Famara**, until coming to a junction by a scruffy house with a wine press (Wp.6 24M), where the tarmac lane turns right towards the main road, while we carry straight on along a dirt track. Bearing left at a Y-junction 70 metres later, then left again at a T-junction (Wp.7 28M), we are skirting the base of **Montaña Sóo**, our gentle climb bringing us alongside a farm's fence and across a small rise to briefly descend to a Y-junction (Wp.8 42M), 180 metres after leaving the fence of the farm.

Bearing left, we climb through a land of eroded gullies and sand dunes, paralleled by a fainter jeep track on our right, which soon turns away as our sandy track becomes grittier. We climb more steeply to cross a shallow crest, where we go straight on at a staggered crossroads where the left-hand track runs closer to the rim of **Caldera Trasera**, literally a 'rear crater'. More views open up to us as we climb, **Alegranza** and **Montaña Clara** - the islets north of **Graciosa** - come into view. We briefly descend to cross a gully before a steady ascent alongside the crater of **Caldera Trasera** brings us onto a saddle (Wp.9 52M), which opens yet more views to us - now towards **Caleta de Caballo** and **Club La Santa**.

Caldera Trasera from Wp.9

From the saddle, we begin our descent along the track past a small hollow in the rock, to come to a junction, where an amusing sign urges you to leave a tip if you enjoy the view - and what views they are! Down below we overlook our route as it skirts a compound with a display of scrapped cars. Ignoring the left fork to a house, we turn right before turning left 60 metres later at another hairpin bend junction (Wp.10 57M). We pass the scrap-car yard, our track levelling off before resuming the descent.

When the dirt track swings sharp right towards a square plot, we fork left off the bend on a jeep track coupled with a path (Wp.11 64M), which takes us across a rise to descend to a bowl, where we cross a sandy track (Wp.12 66M) emerging from the valley below **Pico Colorado** (the Short version).

Crossing the sandy track, we join a path that traverses the slope on the far side of the bowl. A gentle traversing ascent takes us to reach a crest where we cross a dirt track in sight of the first houses of **Sóo**, between which we come onto tarmac (Wp.13 71M). Keeping straight on at junctions, we follow the street back to Wp.3 (77M), where we bear right to descend to the main road and return to our starting point.

It's well worth strolling through this historic town, first established as a settlement by the island's original inhabitants, the *Majos*. Cobbled streets lead between white buildings, many of which have a long and interesting history. You can visit the rather austere **Palacio Spínola** palace (open daily 9-15.00 entry fee payable) in **Plaza de la Constitución**. There are several churches, monasteries and museums worth a visit, including the prominent parish church, **Iglesia de Nuestra Señora de Guadalupe** (16th century, with numerous later embelishments), and the old **Teatrillo Municipal de Teguise** which first opened its doors in 1825. Many of the old buildings have changed use over the years; ex-convents and erstwhile homes of the rich and influential now serve as art galleries, museums, shops and bar/restaurants while retaining original façades. At its busiest on Sunday mornings, **Teguise** street market is a magnet for both residents and visitors.

Overlooking the town, on top of the peak of **Guanapay** (446 metres) perches the island's oldest castle, the 16th century **Castillo de Santa Bárbara**, rescued from dilapidation to house the **Museo de la Piratería** - piracy museum. Enjoy panoramic views from the peak, or take a look inside. Open 10am - 4pm.

N.B. We have not included GPS information for this walk, as satellite coverage in the narrow streets is unreliable.

Access by car:
Parking in the **Plaza Espínola** and along the main road.

Access by bus:
In addition to the Sunday market day specials (Nºs 11, 12, 13 & 14), Nºs 7, 9& 10 all go from **Arrecife** to **Teguise**.

We suggest beginning this relaxed stroll with refreshments in one of the town's bars. If you arrive early, call in **Cejas Bar/Café** in **Plaza San Francisco**, near the old **Convento de San Francisco** (1534), no longer a convent, now housing Lanzarote's collection of religious art in the **Museo de Arte Sacro**. Leaving the bar, we turn right to walk through the **Plaza San Francisco**. Turning right at the north-east corner brings us onto **Calle Marqués de Herrera**, passing the **Casa del Marqués** on our left, and continuing on the few steps past the narrow street on our left to see the **Teatrillo Municipal de Teguise** which has given service as a church, hospital and children's hospice before becoming a theatre in 1825.

Doubling back, we take the narrow street which runs north on **Calle Espíritu Santo** to the great open space known as **Parque La Mareta**, although there's little evidence of greenery in this large public area. If you are here on Corpus Christi this square is transformed by colourful 'carpets' drawn with coloured salts.

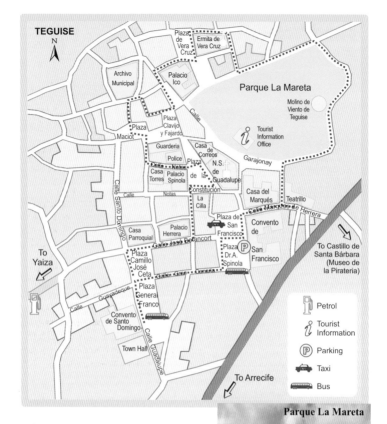

TEGUISE

Plaza de Vera Cruz
Ermita de Vera Cruz
Archivo Municipal
Palacio Ico
Parque La Mareta
Molino de Viento de Teguise
Calle
Plaza Maciot
Plaza Clavijo y Fajardo
Tourist Information Office
Guarderia
Police
Casa de Correos
Casa Torres
Palacio Spinola
Plaza de la Constitución
Plaza N.S. de Guadalupe
Garajonay
Calle Santo Domingo
Calle
Calle
Notas
La Cilla
Casa del Marqués
Teatrillo
Calle Marques de Herrera
Casa Parroquial
Palacio Herrera
Plaza de San Francisco
Convento de
Calle José Betancort
Plaza Dr.A. Spinola
San Francisco
To Castillo de Santa Bárbara (Museo de la Pirateria)
To Yaiza
Plaza Camillo José Ceta
Calle Gran General
Plaza General Franco
Calle Guayadeque
Calle
Convento de Santo Domingo
Town Hall
Calle Guadalupe
To Arrecife

Petrol
Tourist Information
Parking
Taxi
Bus

Parque La Mareta

Following its edge counter-clockwise brings us to a well preserved (except for some graffiti) windmill **Molino de Viento de Teguise**, the last remaining of twelve in this area which were used to grind cereal grains.

El Molino de Viento de Teguise

We continue our circumnavigation of the *parque*, turning off north on the **Plaza Reina Ico** and into **Plaza de Vera Cruz** dominated by the **Ermita de Vera Cruz** with its magnificently huge doors. Leaving the *plaza* by its south-west corner, we walk to the next junction of streets where we go left (S), passing **Palacio Ico** on our left, a former billet for soldiers, easily recognised by its old wooden

Palacio Ico

balcony - rare on a largely treeless island.

Continuing ahead and taking a short dogleg right and left brings us into **Plaza de Clavijo y Fajardo**, where we turn right on a narrow street, at the end of which the **Archivo Municipal** faces us.

Turning left and immediately left again brings us into **Plaza Maciot**, which we walk through to leave by the narrow street in its south-east corner, then taking the next left with **Casa Torres** forming the corner, next door to the seventeenth century **Palacio Spínola** which became a museum in 1984, its walls on this side in the **Calle Notas** looking rather unstable, despite its reputation as the town's most important piece of architecture. We step out into the main cobbled square of **Plaza de la Constitución**, the main façade and entrance to **Palacio Spínola** on its western side, and with the **Iglesia de Nuestra Señora de Guadalupe** on the opposite side, an imposing building standing out from the surrounding austere and simple architectural styles; on its north side is a building that once served as the post office, still known as **Casa de Correos** but now used by the Univerity of Las Palmas de Gran Canaria as a School of Medicine. By the south side of the church, the narrow lane **Calle Zonzamas** leads into the **Parque La Mareta**.

Also look for the seventeenth century **Bankia**, on the southern edge of the square, one of the most attractive banks you are likely to see, housed in the **Cilla de Diezmos y Primicias** building once used to store grain paid as tithes - not too much of a change of use, then.

Cilla de Diezmos y Primicias

We leave the *plaza* by the street at its south-west corner, **Calle León y Castillo**, taking the second right onto **Calle José Betancort**, bringing us past the **Palacio Herrera** on our right - turn right around the building's corner to see its impressive wall plaque before retracing our steps back onto **Calle José Betancort** and continue in a westerly direction, passing the **Casa Parroquial** on our right. Turning left at the end of the street where it meets **Calle Guadalupe** at **Plaza Camillo José Cela** takes us past a small public garden and bus stop, opposite the **Convento de Santo Domingo** (1698), one of the town's largest buildings, and an important centre for local government offices and cultural activities in this region. It also houses the **Centro de Arte Santo Domingo** (open Mon-Fri 10.00 - 15.00, Sun 10.00-14.00). To return to our start point, backtrack to the first street right, **Calle Gran Canaria**, which leads us back to **Plaza Doctor Alfonso Espínola**.

Despite its unpromising name, Malpaso meaning 'bad pass/route', our circular out of **Haría** is a Lanzarote classic combining a hidden *barranco* stuffed with endemic flora and the possibility of seeing running water - a real rarity on Lanzarote - with marvels of the old 'Forgotten Trail' on our return. That's not all, add on the spectacular cliff-top views from **Mirador del Risco de Famara** plus a refreshment opportunity at another *mirador* and the scene is complete for a most memorable adventure.

It's still well within the compass of leisure walkers so if you only have time for one walk in the **Haría** region then make it our 'Barranco del Malpaso'; you won't regret it.

| 3/4 | 2½ H | 9½ km | 350m / 350m | ↻ | 2 |

Access by car: We have three parking options. Park in central **Haría** 200 metres NE of *ayuntamiento*. Park at the sports centre (between Wp.19 and Wp.3), which saves 2kms of street walking. Park out of town at the recreation area by **Mirador del Risco de Famara** off the LZ-10 main road.

Access by bus: N°7 from **Arrecife** calls at **Haría**.

ayuntamiento (town hall) in the centre of Haría

We start out from the small square facing the ayuntamiento in the centre of **Haría** (Wp.1 0M) to stroll along the street (W) to the **Eckhoff** shop (Wp.2 3M) on the corner; **GR131** signpost. Here we turn left onto **Calle Ángel**

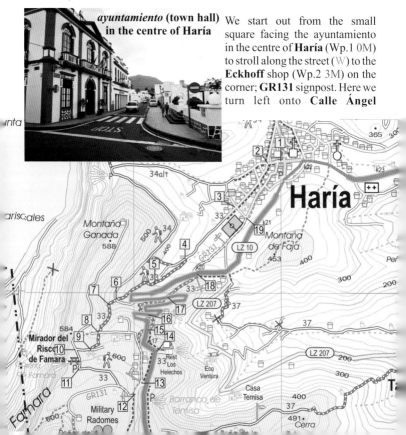

uerra to start heading away from the town (SW), passing a mixture of ouses and plots as we come gently up to pass the sports ground (Wp.3 12M). st the last house we are out into the countryside walking along a dirt track tween stone walled fields and plots while ahead we have the great swoops the LZ-10 framing our return descent on the 'Forgotten Trail'. It's easy olling gently uphill to pass a vineyard with wooden pallet walls before we me up to pass a chained entrance on our right, followed by a solid steel gate ross the main track just after it starts climbing up from the stream (Wp.4 M 359m).

metres before the steel gate we bear left to follow the stream bed. After a w metres of stepping from stone to stone a trail becomes well defined before ssing to the southern side of the stream. It's a narrow single-file path as it mbs above the watercourse for us to push past fennel, agave and intense al endemics, passing another field of vines on our left before our path itches to the opposite side of the stream (Wp.5 30M).

we climb through the endemic flora the terraces gradually change from tivated to abandoned, reverting to nature. Water erosion has narrowed the eady narrow path requiring careful footwork. We keep following the eam, our path widening a bit and running slightly above the watercourse. e path turns away from the stream only to rejoin it 50 metres later before

Ascending the *barranco*

ssing a stone-paved track climbing off he right between stone walls. Sticking he trail alongside the stream, we climb st a 'netted rock' dam to spring onto a ad dirt track (Wp.6 42M) in a U-bend ere a chained track forks off to the ht.

ssing the dirt track, we climb up the rrow stone path between the tercouse and the chained track to pass more dams. After the steep climb to third dam (Wp.7 45M) nestling below lump of trees, our path crosses the ercourse as a sharp turn in the ranco takes **Haría** from sight behind as we climb steeply up past trees to ne up to the remains of a cistern and hut ch mark the upper reaches of the *barranco*. We continue upwards, ivated fields appearing as the *barranco* finishes, our path continuing ill to a dirt track (Wp.8 60M).

oss the track, our path continues up past stone-walled fields before nging right to bring us onto another dirt track and the sight of picnic tables .9 66M); after nearly three hundred metres of climbing ascent its almost divine providence has placed the tables here just for us. It's an easy stroll g (W) to meet the main track (Wp.10) where we turn left to follow the k uphill, military camouflaged radomes coming into view as we reach the access path into the **Mirador del Risco de Famara Área Recreativa** and ar park (Wp.11 74M). In Lanzarote's largest *área recreativa* you'll find a able children's playground along with enough picnic tables to seat the est of extended families, plus of course the *mirador*. Arrive here on a weekend and you'll find the place bustling with Lanzarote families settling in for a day's relaxation complete with catering; on weekdays you could have the whole place to yourself. Missing at any time are tourist hire cars; seemingly this spectacular location is too far from the tarmac for visitors to consider, much to their loss.

From the car park entrance (Wp.11) we still have some gentle uphill along the broad track (E) before we pass a dirt track accessing a building on our left and then come down to a crossroads where we swing left to pass a farm on our left before coming to the tarmac lane (Wp.12 97M) serving the **Ermita de las Nieves**. Joining the **GR131**, our stroll along this section of high ground provides increasing views over the **Haría** valley and east to **Tabayesco**, and there's evidence of cultivation returning to this previously abandoned farming area in the form of new fields and farmhouses under construction. Along the tarmac (NNE) we come to a dirt track (Wp.13) accessing houses before we reach the main LZ-10 road.

If you plan to call at **Rest Mirador Los Helechos**, recommended for its view rather than its cuisine, then continue down to the LZ-10 and carefully walk along the main road to the extensive car park (wildly over-optimistic in size compared to the numbers who call here) (Wp.14 102M). Should you prefer to eschew the restaurant's delights then take the dirt track (N) on the **GR131** route (Wp.13A) that leads down past the wooden cross to the LZ-10.

We always call in at **Restaurant Los Helechos**, really because it's there but also to marvel at this waste of a golden opportunity. At best it's a cafe and gift shop with a massive car park in a spectacular location, after which any description goes as rapidly downhill as the LZ-10. Food and drink seem palatable enough but the café is a depressing monument to featureless formica which even the spectacular view from its windows can't lighten. Its gift shop is a marvel of everything that might possibly count as Lanzarote tat, seemingly displayed on the basis that the visiting tourists will buy anything, at any price, no matter how awful.

On the descent

From **Los Helechos** (0M), we follow the road north, taking care on the section of road walking until after 400 metres we meet the **GR131** donkey trail (Wp.15), then enjoying the wonderful descent, taking extreme care at the road crossings (Wps.16, 17 & 18) to come out on a dirt track running along the valley floor into **Haría**.

We stay on the dirt track which becomes a tarmac street after passing the sports ground junction (Wp.19 35M), then it's César Manrique's house before the houses form up into long terraces, all different so quite the opposite of UK terraces. Easy strolling down the street, passing a couple of side streets and through a wiggle, brings us back onto our outward route at a T-junction just a few metres from our start point in the plaza.

The region around **Haría** contains a diversity of landscapes, ranging from lush valleys to barren hills and an unusual custom built *mirador* that nobody seems to know about. Our route is a complete mixture of a little tarmac, quite a lot of dirt road, a steep climb, a pathless section, breathtaking views; and the pleasure that comes from knowing that you won't have to share any of this with coach parties.

Access by car: Park in **Haría** on the signed large car park, 150 metres NE of our start.
Access by bus: N°7 from **Arrecife** calls at **Haría**.

Short Walk
From the **Eckhoff** collection shop, 150 metres west of the *ayuntamiento*, continue westwards on the street, which becomes the dirt road running up the valley to the *mirador* and return the same way; or extend by following the dirt road from the *mirador* (Wp.13) for the second half of our full route.

We start in the centre of **Haría** opposite **Bar Ney-Ya** (Wp.1 0M). Our first objective is the road junction at the top of the town. We can either walk straight up the **Máguez** road (N), or take the pedestrian street (E) past the church and then turn left (N) up the street; both options deal with the least pleasant part of the route as we slog up narrow streets. Both routes climb up the northern summit of the town, coming together at a junction (Wp.2) from which we head out on a country road on our front left (NW), **Calle Casa Atras**, rather a grand name for a smear of tarmac laid on a dirt road. Leaving the houses behind, we have views across the valley to a large quarry as we stroll down to a junction with a dirt road (Wp.3).

Here we go left (W) on the dirt road, though you could continue down the tarmac into the valley to go left on the next dirt road; it's a slightly longer and

more energetic choice though, and with less extensive views. It's an easy stroll across the southern slope of the valley, passing through a patchwork of neatly cultivated plots and fallow fields being reclaimed by endemic plants.

We stroll past a squat house (Wp.4) surrounded by cultivated plots, and the dirt road becomes less used as we head up the valley. A steep dirt road drops down to the right linking our route with the longer alternative (Wp.5) before we crest a rise, then our road runs gently downhill to a junction with the alternative route (Wp.6). It is noticeable that the valley's southern slopes are more lush than the northern and mostly barren slopes, as we steadily ascend to come up to a breeze-block walled enclosure (Wp.7 33M).

Here we have another choice of route, our official route taking the faint track that climbs steeply up beside the enclosure. Another option is to continue on the dirt road to its end and follow a steep trail up over **Matos Verdes** to join our official route below the peak. The problem with this cliff top route is that it is usually extremely windy on all but the calmest days.

We take the faint track and start climbing steeply - and we do mean steeply - as the slope would benefit from having stairs cut into it.

The summit of the ridge, 40 minutes into the route

A 'puff and grunt' ascent takes us up past the top of the enclosure to reach the summit of the ridge by a gap in a stone wall (Wp.8 40M); after that exertion you have an excuse to stop and take in the extensive views over the **Haría** valley before continuing.

Once through the wall, we swing right to follow it uphill towards a sad and lonely tree-stump, once a palm. The path is so little used we could think of this section as 'open ground' navigation. A small cairn (Wp.9) marks the spot where we move away from the wall and start to cross the long abandoned terraces to another gap in another stone wall (Wp.10). **La Caleta** and **Famara** come into view - and what a view it is - as we cross the terraces to a gap in another stone wall (Wp.11).

As we round the slopes below **Matos Verdes** we maintain altitude as we pass above a large stone storm-water wall which protects the lower valley, before coming to a path (Wp.12 52M) which runs down from the peak along the top of the cliffs; you'll notice that the wind's strength is multiplied here near the cliff edge.

The path at 52 minutes

We pick our way down the path's gritty surface, which improves as we get lower, but it's still wiser to stop if you want to take in the impressive views. Our route runs down to join a dirt road beside an unusual structure (Wp.13 60M).

From above, this roofless structure resembles a very fancy grape vine cultivator, but from close to it is clearly a series of windbreaks for picnickers along with a parking area, so that they can enjoy the *mirador* views with some protection from the high winds; rather a shame that it does not feature on maps or in guide books, as visitors are most unlikely to stumble across this stunning location.

Views over the Haría valley From the *mirador* we have a choice of either short-cutting down the dirt road running down the valley to **Haría**, or taking our official longer route exploring the **Haría** valley. Leaving the *mirador,* we head up the dirt road which runs below the slopes of **Montaña Ganada**. After a steady uphill the gradient eases for easy strolling between abandoned terraces above and below our route, more of **Haría** coming into sight ahead of us.

A pungent whiff announces a goat farm ahead as we pass the first cultivated plots, climbing a rise before the road turns right above the goat farm (Wp.14 74M), giving excellent views over the **Haría** valley. Now it's easy strolling towards **Valle de Malpaso**, our route lined with gigantic prickly pear in places as we walk above neatly cultivated plots to come to a junction at several palms (Wp.15 80M).

Going sharp left, we leave the main dirt track to descend between the plots on a rough track, once a boulder-laid donkey trail but now much eroded and covered in *picón* grit in places, requiring careful footwork on our descent. The track narrows to a trail and then to a path, before it comes down to a trail which runs along the valley floor (Wp.16 88M).

Gratefully, we turn left and head alongside of the stream as the trail runs gently downhill to come onto a dirt track by a steel gate (Wp.17 91M). It's comfortable strolling, crossing a plant-choked watercourse before we reach civilisation in the form of the sports centre football ground (Wp.18), after which the houses start. Continuing down the tarmac street we turn right at its end, by the **Eckhoff** collection shop, and walk along to the **Plaza de la Constitución** and the prospect of an *agua con gas* followed by a cold beer in **Bar Ney-Ya** (110M).

In far distant days **Teguise** was the capital of Lanzarote, and as is the way of things, all routes led to the capital. This long linear route is a relic of those times, when it provided the main route from **Haría** to the capital. Being a ridge-top route, it has survived the depredations of road building largely intact, and its elevation produces many spectacular views. There's a stiff climb through Lanzarote's most floriferous landscape, but you can divert to **Bar/Rest Los Helechos** for refreshments after completing most of the ascent. Once on the ridge - more a wide-backed *lomo* - it's easy striding with stops to take in the awesome cliff-top views. After those views, trailing down into **Teguise** is rather disappointing, but at least it makes for easy walking.

* at start and end of route

Access by car:
Best approach is to park in **Teguise** and then take the N°7 bus to **Haría.**

Access by bus:
N°7 from **Arrecife** calls at **Teguise** on its way to **Haría.** From **Teguise** the N°7, 9 and 10 buses link to **Arrecife**.

From the centre of **Haría** outside **Bar Ney-Ya** on **Plaza de la Constitución** (Wp.1 0M) we go right in front of the *ayuntamiento* to stroll along to take the first street on our left. The small street takes us gently uphill passing a well and César Manrique's house on our right, shortly before the tarmac swings right (Wp.2 10M) towards the sports complex. Here we continue straight ahead, the tarmac changing to dirt as we leave the housing behind.

Ahead, the line of the donkey trail which climbs the ridge at the end of the valley is clearly visible. We stroll along through a bucolic landscape of black picón cultivated plots interspersed with fallow fields populated with endemic flora. Coming to a junction (Wp.3) we take the minor track to our front right. Our stroll becomes more serious as the track steepens into a slogging ascent towards the main road. Where the track swings left up to the tarmac we take a donkey trail straight ahead to climb up onto the road (Wp.4 27M). Carefully crossing over onto our trail's continuation we have a long climbing traverse before meeting the road again (Wp.5 40M). Carefully over the road our trail is into another climbing traverse through the endemic flora.

We come up under buttresses supporting the road, as a hairpin bend in our trail (Wp.6 43M) directs us towards another buttress. We come up to touching distance of the massive wall to zigzag steeply up alongside the tarmac (Wp.7) at a hairpin bend. Our trail, now mostly boulder-cobbled now, climbs steeply up through more zigzags to a hairpin bend (Wp.8) that directs us towards the **Mirador de Haría** building, a climbing traverse leading us up to the road again (Wp.9 48M). Carefully crossing the road, we find our trail's continuation 20 metres uphill where the path climbs up from a red rock dell, soon becoming boulder-laid again. As our trail curves right, we get views down the **Valle de Temisa** as we push our way up through lush plant life to

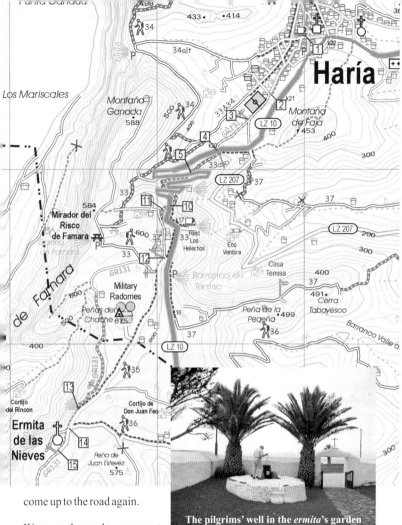

The pilgrims' well in the *ermita*'s garden

come up to the road again.

We cross the road to come onto the faintest section of the trail. Above us is a wooden cross which we use as a direction marker while climbing up over bare rock, before the trail resumes to take us past the cross (Wp.10). Twenty metres after the cross there is faint (easily missed) junction (Wp.11 55M) where we continue gently uphill to come onto a dirt road. We go left to follow the dirt road along to join the **Ermita de las Nieves** tarmac lane (Wp.12) beside the LZ-10 main road.

We have an easy stroll along the narrow lane, ignoring a track to our front right, and passing the radar station entrance, with views opening up to our left (E) over the main road and down to the coastal plain. Over a small crest, and now the *ermita* comes into view ahead of us. This is easy striding country, so you might care to divert right to a *mirador* viewpoint at the top of the cliffs (Wp.13). Before we reach the *ermita* a lane joins from the left (Wp.14); our 'Mala to Teguise' route. Another 300 metres sees us arrive at the *ermita*'s walled courtyard (Wp.15 90M), where we take shelter from the wind inside its walled garden.

ERMITA DE LAS NIEVES

17th century **Ermita de las Nieves** (Chapel of the Snows) stands in isolation at Lanzarote's coldest, windiest and most exposed spot; visitors can shelter inside its surrounding walls, an oasis of relative calm away from the ferocity of the elements within which a garden thrives. Pilgrims of all sorts have paused here over the centuries, whether seeking spiritual sustenance or the quenching of thirst from its drinking water supply, though we can't vouch for its potability. The *ermita* itself is open on Saturdays (14.30 -18.00) and on 5th August, its Saint's day.

The views from the cliffs near the *ermita* shouldn't be missed, but take great care, especially on windy days (unfortunately, in the majority). **Playa de Famara** lies below, while the island of **La Graciosa** will be visible on a clear day to your right, beyond the **Risco de Famara** cliff. You may also make out the further islands of **Montaña Clara** and beyond that, **Isla de Alegranza** when visibility allows. The highest point on the island (670 metres) is **Peñas del Chache** to the north-north east, standing 70 metres higher than the *ermita* and occupied by a military installation, so is off limits to visitors.

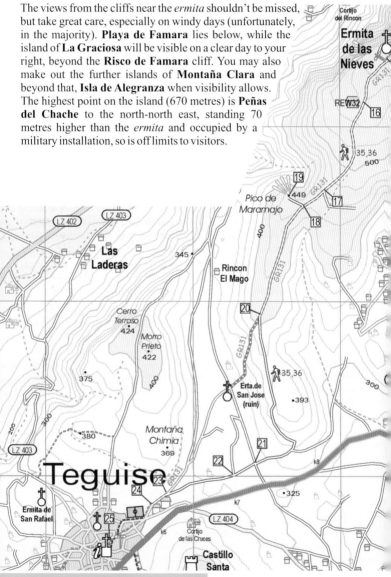

From the **Ermita de las Nieves,** our route could not be more straightforward. We simply stroll south-west on the dirt road, passing 'REW32' (Wp.16), another military compound with aerials.

The dirt road, little-used by vehicles, makes for easy strolling as it runs gently downhill along the broad backed *lomo*; for more imposing views we can always divert right to the cliff top. We pass a track off to the left (Wp.17) before coming to a junction (Wp.18) where we go right to a *mirador* viewpoint overlooking a sharp cleft in the cliffs (Wp.19); beautiful views and even equipped with seat-height rocks to relax on.

... views, views ...

Coming back to the main track we continue gently downhill with **Castillo de Santa Bárbara** dominating the view ahead. Our route curves towards the south and the first buildings of **Teguise** come into view. The **GR131** goes off on a trail to our right (Wp.20), giving us an alternative descent off the *lomo*.

A black *picón* field stands out against the barren landscape, just before a small uphill section, after which our track starts to run down off the *lomo* towards a patchwork of cultivated fields, then curving down to a cross-roads of tracks (Wp.21). The main road is away on our left as we go straight ahead on the narrower track running between the plots directly towards the town. We pass a track off to the right (Wp.22) before strolling up behind the first buildings of the town at a track junction (Wp.23) where we rejoin the **GR131** and then reaching the football ground (Wp.24) where we finally come onto town streets. Keeping the church tower as our direction finder we stroll down the quiet streets (on weekdays at least) to arrive in the main square (Wp.25).

Another of Lanzarote's classic walking routes, all of which is on well stabilised dirt tracks or tarmac. The second half of the route, from **Ermita de las Nieves**, is common to Walks 35 and 36, so is not repeated again here. Our personal preference is for our 'Haría-Teguise' route as the initial ascent simply melts away, but here it is always staring you in the face all the way up to the ridge; but it is 'horses for courses' and we accept that you might prefer the **Mala** approach to **Ermita las Nieves**.

* in **Teguise**

Access by bus:
N°7 and N°9 buses from **Arrecife** to **Mala** (via **Teguise**). Alight at the *correos*, then walk along the old main road (N) for 250 metres and just past the village school our route starts at the tarmac lane on the left (Wp.1).

Access by car:
2CSK Route. Park off the old main road in **Mala**, but on the main road in **Teguise**; it's easier to find a car on the main road than in the town streets.

Short Walk. To **Ermita de las Nieves** and return (3½ hours) and you get the benefit from your climb on the downhill return.

Before starting out, it's a good idea to make sure you're equipped for this energetic climb up to the ridge. It's a long ascent of 2 hours plus and 600 metres, climbing almost every step of the way after a deceptively easy start.

From the old main road (Wp.1 0M) we walk up the tarmac lane, keeping right to pass in front of **Ermita de las Mercedes** where our lane swings left to head across the plain towards the distant ridge. The new LZ-1 road presents no difficulty as our route climbs gently up to a bridge over the LZ-1 (Wp.2). Over

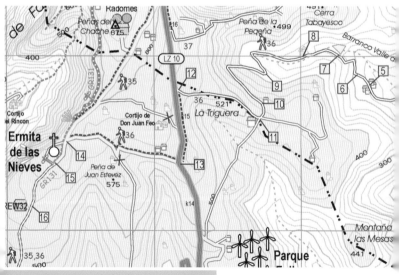

the bridge, and we are heading towards rural tranquility as we come up to a pair of houses at a junction and take the right hand track (Wp.3).

We're now climbing steadily up the side of a valley to go through a hairpin bend across its watercourse which gives us views back over our outward route, and the fields devoted to the *tunera* cactus and their 'crop' of Cochineal beetle which are still cultivated in this region. We come up onto the line of the ridge and a junction beside a ruin (Wp.4 26M) where a track goes off to our

Cochineal farming

right. There is still plenty of climbing to come, so you might want to take a break by walking out along the track to see the **Presa de Mala** dam, only containing water after wet weather.

From the *presa* junction we continue up the track toward a distant hamlet, the ground around our route deeply scarred by storm water erosion, in contrast to the massively walled terraces along this section. A steady ascent brings us up to the hamlet (Wp.5 44M) to walk past an impressive stone wall (Wp.6) and the radomes come into view; known locally as the 'golf balls'. With the cliff wall at the head of the **Barranco Valle del Palomo** looming ahead of us, we start slicing our route up into our 'one step after another' approach with a dam in the *barranco* floor (Wp.7) giving us the chance for a 'Look at that' breather. Passing a ruin (Wp.8) gives another excuse, as does a small bridge (Wp.9 71M). Cultivated plots enclosed by well built walls have relieved the ascent so far, but there is no denying that it is uphill and more uphill as our track zigzags up for us to reach a small house with an interesting back garden (Wp.10 88M).

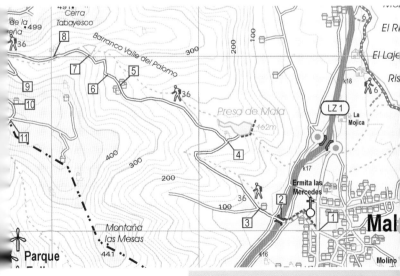

At last the gradient eases as we come up to a white building set alongside a five-way junction (Wp.11) to the north of the **Parque Eólico** wind farm. Turning right to pass in front of the building, we have the luxury of a gentle uphill stroll to come onto the LZ-10 road (Wp.12 105M), facing the radomes set on **Peñas del Chache**. Turning left down the road we head towards the wind farm to take the lane on the right (Wp.13) signed to the **Ermita de las Nieves**. Up the lane, we wriggle through a zigzag before coming up to meet the dirt track of Walk 35 (Wp.14). Left up the tarmac, or along the dirt track that runs around the western side, brings us up to a well earned break at the island's best known *ermita* (Wp.15 132M).

Ermita de las Nieves (Chapel of the Snows) is a popular stopping off point for both walkers and drivers, and could be idyllic, if only someone would put in a little *típico* bar to cater for the many visitors.

If you've made the climb in hot weather (What other sort is there on Lanzarote?) you'll appreciate the cool shade given by the courtyard walls; before leaving, stroll west across the parking area to the edge of the escarpment for the best views down over **Famara** and **La Caleta**.

Our second stage of the route into **Teguise** is identical to Walk 35. GPS users should note that waypoints 14 to 25 are common to both routes.

Famara and La Caleta, far below

The authorities have removed the big red & white mast along with moving the rubbish bins making our original route a tad confusing so we have rerouted the tricky pathless section in the first leg of this adventurous route to make it easier to follow - as easy as possible, that is. Starting in **Tabayesco** at a PR signpost, you might think it is simply following the PR-LZ 01 official trail until joining the dirt track at Wp.6; it might be 'official' but it is largely pathless - even if 'signed' at some junctions - so that without a detailed walk description, and possibly GPS, innocents relying on the official signage could easily find themselves in difficulties.

The pathless section at the start, if walked clockwise, will not be a problem for experienced walkers; we don't recommend walking this route in reverse.

4/5   3H   11 km   540m / 540m   0*

* divert to **Restaurante Los Helechos** (from Wp.12, 2 star)

Access by car:
From the LZ-1 turn off onto the LZ-207 to drive up to the start in **Tabayesco** where we park on the straight section of the road before the church, 100 metres before our start at the **Centro Cultural** junction.

Access by bus:
Route Nºs 7 & 9 call at the LZ-207 junction off the LZ-1, adding an extra 1.5km (one-way) along the not very frequented road to reach the start in **Tabayesco** village.

Wp.1, our peak visible on the right

Our start is at the crossroads 60 metres past the church at a PR-LZ signpost and **Centro Cultural** on the corner (Wp.1 0M). **Calle La Luciana**, our return route, comes from below on our right as we set off to climb along the LZ-207 road, to pass the village name sign, before going through a double bend. In the second hairpin bend, we join a walled sloping plot at the end of which (Wp.2 9M) we bear left and climb steeply along its stone wall (WSW).

Already virtually pathless, we swing left around the upper corner of the stone wall to traverses the slope, shadowing the upper wall of the field until reaching a big cream-and-ochre-coloured crack (Wp.3 13M) in the ground, just a few metres past the end of the wall. We turn right and climb steeply, following this gully, which will be our main guidance for now. When the gully splits to form a big 'Y' letter, we stay inside of the 'Y'. Sticking to the broad ridge line, we head towards an outcrop visible on the ridge ahead of us.

Reaching the outcrop (Wp.4 25M), views of more terraces open above us as we climb into view of a ruined hut on the ridge - our next objective. Toiling up steadily to steeply, we stay on the ridge line, guided by the ruin and also the main peak of the ridge, **Cerro Tabayesco**, which gradually comes into sight.

From the ruin (Wp.5 33M), we could continue climbing straight ahead, but a more comfortable ascent is to bear left across the slope (S) for 100 metres, before turning right (W) to resume our steady pathless climb.

Clambering between gullies and remains of terraces, we are guided by the highest rocky outcrop of **Cerro Tabayesco**. As we steadily approach the outcrop we come to a faint jeep track which, as it curves up through a U-bend, becomes a clear dirt track (Wp.6 43M) under cultivated plots nestling below **Cerro Tabayesco**. This marks the end of the 'pathless open ground' navigation section of our route.

The waypost at Wp.8

With all the difficult, pathless navigation and major ascent behind us, we can indulge in the luxury of relaxed walking while taking in the impressive views over the **Tabayesco** valley as we stroll along the track amongst the plots to cross a saddle between the two peaks (Wp.7 47M). The track brings us to the surprising sight of a PR-LZ waypost below three palms (Wp.8 56M) at 459m altitude saying that **Tabayesco** is 2.2km behind us; how the authorities know this is a mystery as we can't imagine any official who has followed our route (the only safe route) having the temerity to recommend it as an 'official PR-LZ route'.

The waypost is on a junction with a track forking left (E) onto **Peña de la Pequeña** as we follow the main track (W) downhill past a cabin and cultivated plots to another low point of the promontory, which also narrows so that as we climb up the track past ruins of cottages, we get views down onto our Walk 36

route climbing up the **Presa de Mala** valley. It's a rather steep ascent up the track to bring the radomes back into sight, as we come up to cultivated plots and cabins which we pass on our right as we approach the LZ-10 main road. Just as it seems we're going to step onto the road, our track turns right, paralleling the road for a short section before we step onto the tarmac (Wp.9 79M).

Walking on the left side of the road, we stroll past the 16km marker for the 600 metres that brings us to the *mirador* car parking and a pavement (Wp.10 88M). From the end of the *mirador* we turn left onto the **Ermita de las Nieves** lane and then immediately right onto a dirt track (Wp.11 91M) which after a few metres joins the **GR131**. From here we simply follow the **GR131** to pass an electricity pylon, 90 metres after which we take the trail off the track (Wp.12 98M) that leads down past a wooden cross to cross the LZ-10 onto the donkey trail, taking care on all three of the road crossings, until we come to the LZ-10 for one last time (Wp.13 116M).

wooden cross after Wp.12

On the LZ-10 we turn right to pass the 20km marker, for the 400 metres downhill until we turn right onto the LZ-207 **Tabayesco** road (Wp.14 122M). Walking down the road, we step off onto a jeep track, accessing plots and a hut away on our left, just before the road's crash barrier starts. It is a picky descent on the rough track until it turns left, where we step off the track down onto a narrow walking trail (Wp.15 125M). From the top of the trail we have superb views over the final section of our route from the bowl at the head of the valley, down to **Tabayesco** and the Atlantic Ocean. Our narrow trail winds its way steeply down into the head of the valley including a section of zig-zags before we emerge below the topmost cultivated plots on a dirt track (Wp.16 135M).

We turn left to head down the track, easy strolling after the slightly picky descent on that interesting trail, passing a farmstead's noisy dogs and chickens. Ignoring minor tracks to left and right we arrive at a major track junction (Wp.17 145M) where we keep left following the valley's watercourse.

Our final section is easy strolling along the valley floor between a mixture of *malpaís* and cultivated plots. Ignoring obvious side tracks, we pass a stone hut neatly built into a terrace on our right, then a track left to a house with a lush green garden hidden by trees. Passing **Finca Natura** with its palm-lined access track we come onto the end of a village street (Wp.18 173M) in **Tabayesco**. After 130 metres, we bear right at a T-junction into **Calle La Luciana**, along which we climb back to our starting point (177M).

This interesting circular route takes in bucolic farmland, upland meadows, stunning cliff-top views, a peak and one of Lanzarote's most impressive *calderas*; only refreshments are missing. Ascents are never steeper than steady, and the range of landscapes and views makes even these seem relatively gentle.

The unorthodox circular shape of the route with a couple of diversions allows you to tailor the route to your choice, skipping one or both (see Short version) of the diversions. Needless to say, it would be a shame as the whole route is exciting!

Access by car: take the **Guinate** road off the LZ-201 and turn left after 430 metres at a Y-junction, taking the church lane. Drive past the church until the end of tarmac to park at the **Centro Socio Cultural**.
Access by bus: no bus connection.
Short version: Omit the two diversions off the main circuit, and bear right at Wp.4 or Wp.6, though you'll miss some of the most interesting features (4km, Ascents/Descents 150 metres).

We start off by the **Centro Socio Cultural** (Wp.1 0M), taking the dirt track

our start at Wp.1

(W), passing cultivation and a fenced *finca* on our right. After a small dirt turning circle, we pass a branch track to the right (Wp.2 7M) leading to abandoned houses at the foot of the ridge - this is our return route, which we have a good chance to scan from here: the ridge path descends following the line of the crest before joining the end of the track at the abandoned houses.

Keeping straight on, we follow the track into the valley past cultivated *picón* plots, before passing house N°16 with a decorative well on our right, then a

junction at Wp.2

Wp.4, short option path

farm with a palm-lined driveway on the left. After 250 metres we bear right at a Y-junction (Wp.3 22M), the left branch leading to a cluster of palms. We continue climbing gently and as we near the head of the valley, we pass a 30-metres long stripped layer of eroded soil and sediments, after which a path (Wp.4 29M) branches off sharp right. This is our Short walk option; if you opt

r the short version but find this path too steep here, another option to join the lge path is to turn right at Wp.6.

r dirt track curves left at the head of the valley, great views opening up as e climb between old terraces and past a house to a track junction (Wp.5 M), where we turn right.

st past the junction we pass a pair of pits, the **Fuentes de Gayo**, beside a left-nd track before reaching a Y-junction where we take the left fork; the two cks soon coming together again. A valley drops steeply down on our right we continue uphill to the top of the cliffs (Wp.6 42M); take care if you proach the cliff edge as the winds are powerful. Here our return route ntinues to the right, briefly across open ground.

now have two interesting diversions as part of our main itinerary, so we y on the track as it undulates along (SE) away from the cliffs to pass a faint ck off to our right opposite a turning loop before reaching a junction (Wp.7 M) at **Gayo** plateau, where two parallel tracks fork off to the right (notice

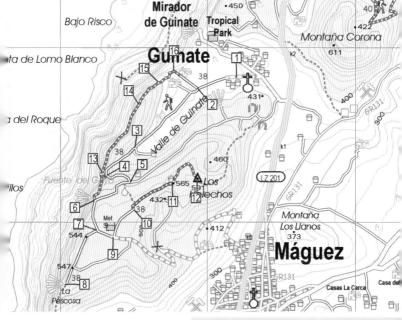

board). Here we take the first track right (WSW) heading for the cliff tops - [...] you think the views from close to the junction can't be topped, you are in for [...] surprise a few minutes later. We walk up past fields cut out of the meadows [...] come up onto the headland.

This track ends at a storm-eroded area where we find a decorative black sto[...] with a spiral, adorned with plants (Wp.8 60M) from where we take [...] impressive views down over **Risco de Famara** to **La Caleta** and the pla[...] beyond.

Back at the main track (Wp.7 73M) we head (ESE) past a whi[...] meteorological station, where the track becomes tarmacked, to a juncti[...] (Wp.9 76M) at the end of the station's fence, where a track goes left (NNI[...] Taking to the track for our second diversion we climb up onto a broad back[...] ridge which although only a few metres above our earlier route is almo[...] barren with the exception of a black *picón* field. We walk along the rou[...] track to swing left and right beside the field enclosed by a low stone w[...] (Wp.10 82M). 10 metres before the end of the field our track curves aw[...] before passing several 'minicraters'.

Ahead, the track leads us up the slope to the transmitter hut sitting on the top[...] **La Quemada**, views opening up down over the **Valle de Guinate** from [...] saddle before walking up to the hut (Wp.11 90M). From the antenna peak, [...] follow the initially faint, then well-trodden path (NE) curving east bef[...] bearing right at a junction for a final slog (SE) up to the trig point at the top [...] **Helechos** volcano (Wp.12 100M). This is literally the high point of our ro[...] from where - apart from enjoying the awesome views - we can see messag[...] and signs of stones left on the *caldera* floor. Whipped by the wind we leave [...] summit by retracing our steps back to Wp.6 (130M).

Back at Wp.6, we step off the track to skirt the edge of the cliff (NE), more [...] less pathless, until we see the clear traversing path gently climbing to the [...] of the ridge. We come to a promontory, from which we follow a faint p[...] briefly down to join the main path on the highest of the terraces. Pas[...] junction where the short option path joins us from our right (Wp.13 135M) [...] traverse the grandstand-like slope, the gentle climb taking us up onto the ri[...] plateau, bringing **Graciosa** into view. Once again enjoying hard-to-b[...] views, we follow the broad ridge top to pass a big cairn on a rock shelf, [...] metres short of a Y-junction (Wp.14 149M) where the until-now-barren ri[...] becomes dotted by shrubs.

A big arrow of stones points out to the right, but both branches rejoin a [...] minutes later, so we pick the left fork for a descent along the ridgeline to en[...] more of the ocean-side views. It's a picky descent on a stone-littered path[...] we catch glimpses of the abandoned houses below us at the foot of the ri[...] before bearing right in front of a rock outcrop. Our path becomes m[...] obvious, being marked by cairns now and then, before the branch path fr[...] the arrow-marked junction joins us from our right. We descend past a sr[...] viewing 'platform' (Wp.15 155M), then a second one before being joined [...] another path from the right to cross a colourful bare rock section. We co[...] down to the abandoned houses (Wp.16 160M), to the right of which we [...] their access track. Following this dirt track amongst the old farmlands, [...] stroll to the junction at Wp.2 (165M) and back to our starting point.

Yé is a sleepy farming village far removed from the excesses of Lanzarote's beach resorts. In addition to its rural tranquility, it boasts the most unusual *típico* bar on the island in the **Centro Socio Cultural de Yé** alongside the main bus stop; do call in for coffee and admire the wall murals. Most visitors who discover **Yé** are simply passing through on their way to the 'pay on entry' sanitised **Mirador del Río**; once a simple gun emplacement.

Less well known and largely undiscovered by the casual visitor is the mirador overlooking the **Salinas del Río**, the oldest salt pans of the archipelago dating back to the indigenous islanders and used until the 1970s. You'll not only enjoy similar views, but you'll be in the unusual situation of seeing your whole walking route laid out in front of you before you start out. The route is historicaly known as **Camino de los Gracioseros**; it was an ancient route linking **Isla Graciosa** with Lanzarote in times before the regular maritime service. It was frequently taken by the women of **Graciosa** who were sailed by their men across the strait before climbing the steep donkey trail, heavily loaded with fish, in order to exchange them for other products in the markets of **Haría**. The route was also sought for collection of orchil, a dye obtained from lichens found in abundance on the steeper escarpments.

Even if you don't plan to walk the **Salinas del Río** walk, you must take the easy stroll to the *mirador* (Wp.2) if your visit to Lanzarote is to be complete.

4 | 3 H | 9.5 km | 440m / 440m | 0

Access by car: From **Máguez**, drive past the **Guinate** junction, and turn off the main road 1.7 kilometres further on, onto a narrow lane at **Las Rositas**. Drive carefully down the lane until the imposing **Finca La Corona** is on your right, and then turn left just after the *finca* onto a stone-flagged road which widens into a car park.

Access by bus: not feasible by bus.

mirador view at Wp.2

From the car park (Wp.1 0M) we walk along the paved path past pleasant rocky scenery before starting to drop down a staired descent, views opening up over the straights to **Isla Graciosa**. The stairs bring us to a stone built mirador by an electricity pylon (Wp.2). Along with the beautiful views this is also our decision point. Far below us are the multi-hued *salinas* salt pans, while the path drops straight down the cliffs; an intensely steep descent requiring careful footwork on the zigzagging trail, and an equally intense 'puff & grunt' ascent on our return.

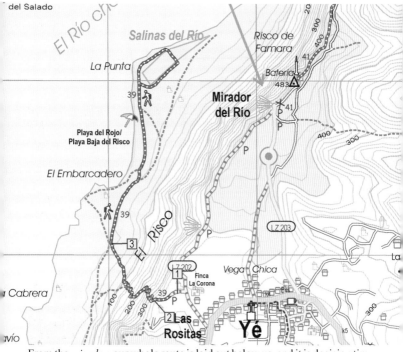

From the *mirador*, our whole route is laid out below us, and it is decision time. This is easily the steepest descent and ascent on the island, requiring concentration all the way down. Concentrating on where you are putting your feet helps combat any sense of vertigo, as does facing the cliff when taking breaks. However if it is windy, or any sign of bad weather, we would suggest you save this route for another day.

We set off, stepping down through the small, steep zigzags in a near vertical descent. This continues down for over a hundred metres before there is any relaxation on a moderate slope, and then we tackle a second series of small, steep zigzags for another hundred metres of near-vertical descent. Finally, our trail comes to a steady descent and passing a fainter trail going left, we keep straight on. Easy walking brings us down to a crossroads with a track (Wp.3 48M).

Having made the descent, we are now free to explore the beach and salt pans, either by keeping to the track (N) or using the tracery of small paths that have been walked. The track ends at an electricity transformer that sends power over to **La Graciosa** via a sea bed cable. **Salinas del Río** is no longer in production, but at least its 'pans' are still here, and the evaporating sea water creates some beautiful colours.

At some stage we have to remember that civilisation in the form of our car is at the top of that cliff. Personally we prefer the ascent to the knee-jarring descent despite its 'puff & grunt' nature requiring a lot of recovery stops, but like it or hate it, it has got to be climbed. At least, when we get back to the *mirador* we certainly have a well-earned sense of achievement, having completed this spectacular route.

Approach the north of Lanzarote and one thing stands out - **Montaña Corona**, the classic volcanic cone peak that dominates the view ahead as you leave **Máguez**. Our short tour visits the northern rim for a peek into the *caldera* before returning to the village via a labyrinth of volcanic vineyards. If you are in **Yé** in the afternoon hours, don't miss the opportunity to visit the unique social centre theatre and bar for a surprise refreshment stop ending to the expedition.

| 2 | 1 H | 3.5 km | 140m / 140m | ↻ | 3* |

*in **Centro Socio Cultural de Yé** though they're not always open

Access by car:
Park in **Yé** church's extensive car park - avoid religious fiestas.

Access by bus: Not suitable for bus access.

Corona seen from Wp.1

We start from the church car park entrance (Wp.1 0M) to walk along the road (E) for 150 metres where, just after the Km4 road marker, we take a dirt track (Wp.2 2M) heading (S) towards the mountain. Our track winds gently uphill through a *zoco*-cultivated area, grapes and almonds, side tracks accessing the fields as we steadily close with **Montaña Corona**.

Gradually, cultivation gives out (Wp.3 10M) as we continue gently uphill through abandoned fields and a shallow valley before ascending through lazy zigzags until our track runs out close to the mountain base (Wp.4 18M). A walking trail continues up past the end of the *zocos* to a stately palm where our narrow trail starts a more serious ascent through endemic plant life, passing a

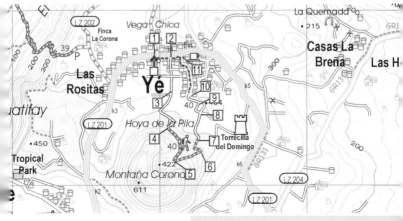

approaching the rim of the caldera, Wp.5

trail coming in from our right before going through a stone wall to continue up to the edge of the mountain's caldera (Wp.5 30M).

It's an impressive *caldera*, the cone's southern section intact as seen in the view from **Máguez**, while the northern rim has collapsed giving us a 'rim-edge' view down to the caldera floor - don't go too close to the edge as the rocks are undercut - more collapses can be expected at any time!

descending towards Torrecilla

From the *caldera* we follow a trail (E) alongside an old stone wall, descending towards the white tower of **Torrecilla del Domingo** visible below us in the distance. We negotiate abandoned terraces, clambering from level to level through, and round, the vigorous plant life including prickly pear! Shadowing the stone wall, our path brings us to a farm's metal fence with a locked gate (Wp.6).

Going left, we skirt the fence, rounding its corner to come through a ruined wall before emerging onto a dirt track at the farm's main entrance gate (Wp.7 40M). Following the track (NW), another dirt track soon joins us from our right just before going through an intersection of sturdy stone walls, 220 metres after which we come to a crossroads of tracks (Wp.8 45M). Bearing left, we go towards an electricity pylon/line. Our track swings right and comes to a T-junction (Wp.9 47M), bringing a white transformer tower into sight; the tower is our way into the village.

We turn left, then right at a crossroads 130 metres later before reaching a garden wall of a first house of **Yé**. Following the fence to the right for 30 metres, we find a narrow dirt path around a big opuntia, which takes us to the end of a tarmac street (Wp.10 51M) near an electricity pylon. Past the transformer tower, we stroll down **Calle El Tefio** onto the main road (Wp.11 58M).

Back to the church (62M) is to the left, but once here, do check the unique establishment of **Centro Socio Cultural**, 40 metres to the right (E). Inside is a theatre setting with wall murals and a café, and when we've found it open on all previous visits we were assured that all visitors will be most welcome - though a little bit of Spanish helps.

Our very last walk is a short but exciting excursion to the island's wind-swept northern-most promontory. César Manrique's unique architecture combined with stunning views from his **Mirador del Río** makes for a special experience. If you are like us, you will want to leave the chattering picture-eager hordes behind and set off along the promontory to take in the spectacular views away from the crowds. For a little effort we are rewarded by jaw-dropping views to **Isla Graciosa**, and if you make it to the end, views expand to the eastern side too. The plus side of the walk is that you can turn back whenever you think you have had enough. The views are however so hypnotizing that before you know it you'll come down to the promontory's end with the needle-sharp spires of the northern tip of the island in front of you.

The **Famara** cliffs are sheer, but the ridge we follow is broad so we never have to walk close to the rim unless you want to, therefore no vertigo risk. Just be sure not to be too close to the wind-swept edge as sudden gusts can occur.

* at **Mirador del Río** Café

Access by car: park at the César Manrique's **Mirador del Río** car park or just below on the supplementary dirt parking, at the northern end of the LZ-202/203 roads.

Access by bus: no bus connection.

Mirador del Río car park, Wp.1

curve east 50 metres after our start

We start from the **Mirador del Río** car park (Wp.1 0M) to stroll south along the LZ-203. In 50 metres we start to curve east, our dirt track separating the gully-strewn slope on our left from a meadow on our right. The dirt track passes an earthwork (E) and joins an electricity line before bringing us to a T-junction (Wp.2 5M) next to a badly eroded gully.

We go left to pass under the power cables to climb gently on the access track for the transmitter before bearing straight ahead at a junction with three concrete structures, where a track forks off to the right. This track goes to the promontory, which is our objective, but it is more interesting to follow the edge of the NW-facing cliff, so we go straight to the trig point (Wp.3 12M), before passing the transmitter and simply skirt the edge of the sharp escarpment. We go NE, keeping a safe distance from the cliffs.

Our pathless descent along the rim brings the promontory into our view before negotiating a big crack in the dry earth, 30 metres after which we come to an underground bunker. Maintaining direction, we pass a small shelter (Wp.4 21M), an old lookout watching over the strait between **Graciosa** and Lanzarote. Passing another underground bunker we come to join the track (Wp.5 28M) that branched off before the transmitter. Now we are rewarded with eastern views towards **Órzola**. We follow the track until it runs out at the end of the broad plateau of the promontory (Wp.6 29M), beyond which it becomes dangerously narrow. After admiring the jagged rock spires of the island's northern-most tip we return to our car (73M); for our return we can either follow the dirt track or the cliff route past the bunkers.

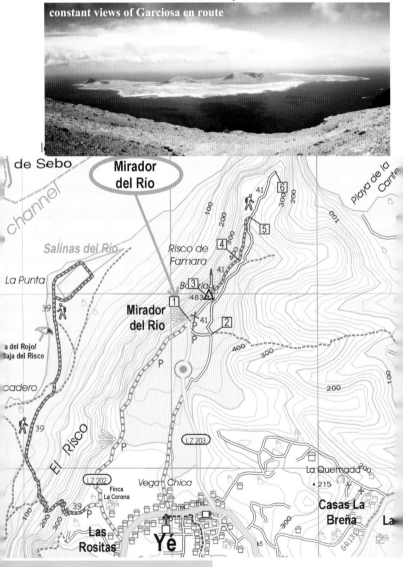

constant views of Garciosa en route

Discovery Walking Guides is a business but it's also a passion for us. Really we are a 'Happiness' organisation hoping to bring you happiness through using the outdoor adventures in our 'Walk!' books and 'Tour & Trail' maps. Our objective is to give you reliable, recreatable walking adventures that you can enjoy. Your happiness is our happiness.

You are our most valuable resource for keeping us up to date with how our books and maps are performing. We want to hear from you; praise is always welcome but some of our best improvements have come from criticism. Criticism can be hard to take, but we recognise that your observations and opinions are valuable if we are to produce better books and maps in the future.

If you discover that things have changed since a 'Walk!' book or 'Tour & Trail' map was published let us know. If you think we could do things better, please let us know.

We receive a lot of emails from our DWG 'family', all of them valuable and all of them replied to as soon as possible.

Send us your updates, praise, criticism and ideas at:

ask.discovery@ntlworld.com

Sometimes serendipity is at work, as happened just as were about to go to print with this book when we received an email that neatly encapsulated our DWG mission statement:-

"Hi David and Ros,
I just want to say a big thank you to you for producing the guide and the map. Absolutely brilliant. (Lanzarote)
My wife Jan and I started visiting the Canaries 21 years ago. At that time we had young sons so we spent our time in the resorts. As they got older we retuned on our own and being keen walkers started to do some walks. This was about 15 years ago. Unfortunately, there were no suitable maps available on the island and I felt we needed a book of walks with maps to see what was out there. It was very confusing landscape and hardly any signposting then. (It is still limited).Fortunately one winter evening back in the U.K. I came across your guide and map which we bought. We booked our winter break in Lanzarote and started to explore. What a joy it has been. Not only have we done most of the walks but as we have got to know the island and the terrain we have been able to modify walks and even do some of our own.
We have also visited Tenerife and used your guide and map for that island. Again excellent. It would be helpful if the map covered the whole island rather than just parts but I presume this is due to size of the island.
We have been to Lanzarote or Tenerife once or twice a year for the last 15 years and I cannot fault the guides or maps. They have greatly enhanced our enjoyment of walking the islands. Without them we would not have ventured into what has been a dramatic landscape with fabulous views. A lot of the time we see few other walkers.
When you next go to Lanzarote there is a walk we discovered which you might like to try. I expect you have had a look at it but if you have not here are the details. I could outline it on a section of your map but I see you do not take attachments unless under a special arrangement. If you would like me to do this please let me know."

To see what became of James & Jan's prosed walking route read on . . .

42 James & Jan's Quemada Circular

This is what happens when least expected. A neat circular route with the option to visit Casitas de Femés plus sampling the bars/cafes in Playa Quemada after completing this scenic adventure. We walk on well defined tracks and trails, with a little bit of tarmac in the villages, so abig thank you to J&J for providing the directions. We have included gps waypoints for the route but these are plotted using the digital map, as compared to our usual recording while walking the route, so treat as approximate on your gps.

3/4 | 3 H | 11 km | 430m / 430m | 3*

* in Playa Quemada

Access by Car:
Park at the end of the LZ-706 at the entrance to the village and walk in to our start at the dirt track (Wp.1).

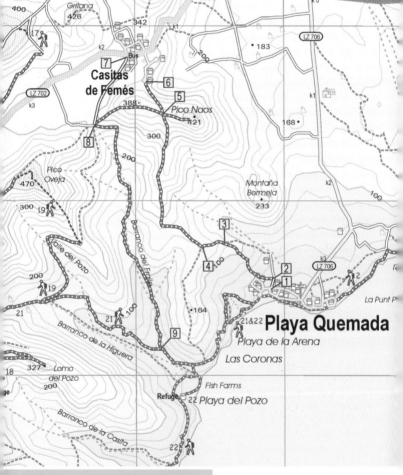

"When you next go to Lanzarote there is a walk we discovered which you might like to try. I expect you have had a look at it but if you have not here are the details." Well, better than just 'try it' we are sharing it in James' own words with just a few embellishments by David & Ros.

It starts at Playa Quemada. Park near the entrance to the village and walk in. *You leave by the white track on your map* (Wp.1) *which runs north but almost immediately turn left on a track* (Wp.2) *not shown on your map.* See map section opposite. Note that the irst section of the route is all uphill until we reach the saddle so pace yourself and take rests whenever necessary.

It runs west then north and joins the track (Wp.3) *which is shown on your map by a broken grey line (a continuation of the white track). Follow it west for a short distance. Where it turns south west towards Playa del Pozo there is a fork* (Wp.4) *which leads north west. Take this.* Broken grey line is a trail, White track is a driveable dirt track. While some trails are wide enough to be tracks we classify most as trails on our maps.

At the next junction turn north. You are now running parallel to Barranco del Fraille which lies below to the west. The track climbs steadily up the west side of the spur. It is slightly vertiginous to the west but nothing untoward. I think my trigger is lower than David's- it must be pretty low (David).
The track is clear and reaches a crossroads of tracks on the top (Wp.5).
It has been a long uphill slog to reach the saddle between the height points. If you have had enough uphill then consider taking the trail (W) to '388' and on to Wp.8. If you do descend to the village look out for the 'Mash' style Bell-Huey helicopter garden ornament.

A right turn will take you to the spot height 421 of Pico Naos. Essential for the best views and only a small exertion.
Straight overtakes you down to Casitas de Femes. Left takes you to spot height 388. We partially walk up Pico Naos and then return to the crossroads and drop to Casitas de Femes. Follow the trail down to the village street (Wp.6) then on to turn left on the 'main' road.

We leave by the track running south west (Wp.7) *to reach the junction of tracks* (Wp.8) *where route 19 comes in from Femes. If you had continued past spot height 388 the track would have dropped to this point. There is a clear path coming down.*

At this junction we had a break feeling very pleased with our progress. Now there is a choice. You can either walk down Barranco del Fraille to Playa de Pozo or take the route 19 track to Barranco de la Higuera and down to Playa de Pozo. We did the former but the latter is more interesting but longer.
Note the two routes come together at Wp.9.

From Playa de Pozo it is a pleasant walk along the coast back to Playa Quemada.
From Wp.9 we follow Walk 21's trail down to Playa del Pozo and then back along the coast to Playa Quemada.

It is very unusual for us (DWG) to find a walking route presented with enough detail to publish that route. 'James & Jan's' Playa Quemada route is the first we have taken direct to publication without researching the route ourselves. For once all the ducks lined up in a row as serendipity presented the unique combination of information and opportunity.

If you are thinking of producing a walking route for other walkers here are our DWG guidelines for that research.

Maps Does a map already show the details making up your walking route? In UK you will be using OS maps which have all the walking trails, tracks (drivable), and tarmacked roads, that you will be following. If those details are already on an OS map then describing your route will be straightforward.

Recording Information along the route to help Users.
We use digital voice recorders for our notes as we walk a route. This is quicker and easier than making written notes. After completing the route we can then review the voice records to make a written description of the route.

Pictures are useful if they help people navigate the route.
Carry a digital camera so that you can take pictures of everything you think might be relevant. Your first picture should be one showing the start point of your route. Features identifying locations along your route are much more useful than 'views' from the route. A phone can be used for your pictures but the quality may be marginal if you are publishing your route in printed form.

GPS is a great help in defining your walking route, especially if details of the route are not already shown on an official map, our usual DWG situation. Simply set your gps track record to Auto and record everything that you think might be useful as a waypoint; "Mark" and "Enter" on most gps units.

Compass Directions can be really useful. While we are gps users we recognise the value of giving compass directions, confirmed on a hand held compass, to make sure people are going in the right direction.

Walk at a Reasonable Pace.
Walking routes should be an enjoyable adventure, not a race against time. Most of us walk at between 3 and 5kmh.

Record your Times along your route.
Most walkers have a watch or a phone telling them the time. Few, except gps users, have anything that tells them the distance, so it makes sense to talk about the times taken along your route.

Edit all that Route Information into your Walk Description.
 Make sure that you include all the key decision points where we need to make a choice about which trail/direction to take. It is easier to filter out the information than finding that you are short of key information and need to go back and rewalk your route!

This glossary contains Spanish and Canarian words found in the text (shown in *italics*), plus other local words that you may encounter.

a

abandonado	abandoned
abierto	open
acantilado	cliff
agua	water
agua no potable	water (not drinkable)
agua potable	drinking water
aljibe	sunken water tank
alto	high
aparcamiento	parking
arepa/arepera	deep fried savoury snack/bar specialising in arepas
autopista	main road, motorway
ayuntamiento	town hall

b

bajo	low
barranco	ravine
bocadillo	bread roll
bodegón	inn
buceo	scuba diving

c

cabezo	peak, summit
cabra	goat
café	coffee
caldera	collapsed cone (volcanic area)
calima	suspended dust brought in by hot east winds
calle	street
camino	trail, path, track
camino particular	private road
camino real	old donkey trail (lit. royal road)
carne	meat
carretera	main road
casa	house
casa rural	country house accommodation to let
caserío	hamlet, village
castillo	castle
cementerio	cemetery
centro comercial	shopping centre
cerrado	closed
cerveza (caña, jarra, presión, lata)	beer (small, large, draught, can)
charco	pool
choza	shelter
clínica	clinic, hospital
colmena	bee hive
comida	food

conquistador	conqueror
cordillera	mountain range
correos	post office
cortijo	farmstead
costa	coast
coto privado de caza	private hunting area
Cruz Roja	Red Cross (medical aid)
cuesta	slope
cueva	cave
cumbre	summit

d

degollada	pass
derecha	right (direction)
desayuno	breakfast
desprendimiento	landslide

e

ermita	chapel
Espacio Natural Protegido	protected area of natural beauty
estación de autobus/ guagua	bus station
este	east

f

farmacia	chemist
faro	lighthouse
fiesta	holiday, celebration
finca	farm, country house

g

gasolinera	petrol station
gofio	flour made from roast maize, wheat or barley
guagua	bus
Guardia Civil	police
guía	guide

h

hornito	lava bubble
hostal	hostel, accommodation
hoya	depression (geological)
huevos	eggs

i

iglesia	church
información	information
isla	island
izquierda	left (direction)

j

jameo	volcanic tube
jamón	ham

l

librería	bookshop

llano	plain	*policía*	police
lluvioso	rainy	*postre*	dessert
lomo	broad-backed ridge	*potaje*	thick soup
m		*pozo*	well
Majos/Mahos	Lazarote's original inhabitants	*prohibido el paso*	no entry
malpais	'bad lands' wild, barren countryside	*puente*	bridge
		puerto	port, mountain pass
malvasia	Malmsey grapes and wine	**q**	
		queso	cheese
mapa	map	**r**	
mareta	raised water collection tank	*risco*	cliff
		roque	rock
mariscos	shellfish	*ruta*	route
mercado	market	**s**	
mirador	lookout/viewing point	*salida*	exit
mojo	spicy sauce based on olive oil, tomatoes and chilis	*salinas*	salt pans
		sangría	wine with fruit punch served in a jug of ice
montaña	mountain	*senda*	path, track
museo	museum	*sendero*	foot path
n		*sin salida*	no through road/route
norte	north	*sirocco*	hot, dust-laden wind from Africa
nublado	cloudy		
o		*sur*	south
oeste	west	**t**	
oficina de turismo	tourist office	*tapas*	bar snacks
		té	tea
p		*tienda*	shop
paella	rice dish, usually with seafood or meat	*típico*	traditional bar/eating place
panadería	bakery	*tormentoso*	stormy
papas (small arrugadas	wrinkled potatoes potatoes in their skins cooked in salt water)	*torre*	tower
		tubería	water pipe
		v	
parapente	hang-glider	*valle*	valley
parque eólico	wind farm	*vega*	meadow
pastelería	cake shop	*ventoso*	windy
peligro	danger	*vino (blanco, tinto, rosado)*	wine (white, red, rosé)
pensión	guesthouse		
pescado	fish	*volcán*	volcano
pico	peak	**z**	
picón	black volcanic rock/sand	*zocos*	crescent shaped vine enclosures (as seen in La Geria)
pista	dirt road/track		
pista (forestal)	forest road/track	*zona recreativa*	recreation area
playa	beach	*zumo/zumería*	freshly pressed fruit juice/juice bar
plaza	square		

Lanzarote is a surprisingly varied island; you cycle up steep valleys through green palm trees and black *picón* fields, then head down from the ridge to the coast where the Atlantic bursts onto black lava-cliffs. In winter it's at its most interesting, full of colour as plant life bursts from the otherwise desert-like terrain. It's a great mountain biking destination, both on and off road and perfect for winter training; there's also the sports complex of Club La Santa open all year. Sporting competitions such as Lanzarote Ironman (in May each year) attract more and more participants.

For the mountain biker, Lanzarote can be divided into three regions; the north where you ride along the coast or through steep green valleys, either on quiet country roads or over rocky trails and single tracks; the centre of the island, less hilly - but far away from being flat, and the south which is again steep and very rocky, but less green. This section offers high mountain dirt tracks and gentle gradients along the coast or through lava fields.

- **What the cyclist will find only occasionally** - but usually can avoid - wet conditions.
- **What might surprise you** - going faster climbing up than rolling down - due to the wind.
- **What might amaze you** - stunning views all over the island.
- **What you have to see** - the landscape around Timanfaya National Park - unforgettable!

Other useful information:-
- In winter bring a windbreaker, maybe zip-on-sleeves and you'll need sun protection all year round.
- It's the law to wear a bike helmet on Lanzarote. One will be included in your cycle hire from all reputable rental companies on the island.
- Take your **Lanzarote Super-Durable Tour & Trail Map**
- When riding off-road please respect local signs and don't leave trails or pistes as this can damage the island's delicate ecosystems.
- Be alert to loose or abandoned dogs - they might view you as escaping goats.

If you need any further advice or want to join us on one of our guided rides don't hesitate to contact us via email:

bike@mylanzarote.com info@tommys-bikes.com
info@bikelanzarote.com

Our shops in **Costa Teguise** (**Bike Station** and **Tommy's BIKES**) stock all kind of bicycles individually adjusted to your needs. We carry spares and biking equipment and also offer guided excursions and useful tips. We've been running our bike excursions for many years and we know all the hidden corners of the island. Our team offers you easy rides for the whole family on quiet roads and trails, with loads of information about traditions and local history of Lanzarote as well as hardcore trails for the serious rider. Currently local authorities are designing signposted MTB-routes for Lanzarote - please contact us for the latest news.

Andreas Kern
www.mylanzarote.com   www.tommys-bikes.com

Bus times change; ask for the latest version on arrival. The Biosphere Information Office at the airport usually has free copies or ask in the Tourist Information Offices.

Occasionally buses showing numbers other than that designated for the route will arrive at the stop; ask the driver if he is going to your destination.

Don't rely on catching the last bus back; carry taxi phone numbers and a mobile phone, just in case. Most villages have a public phone, otherwise, try a bar.

Bono bus tickets can be purchased on the buses and offer a 10% discount off the standard fare.

For current information visit: www.arrecifebus.com and Moovit phone app.

Bus Fares to/from Arrecife;
Airport €1.40, Costa Teguise €1.40, Haría €3.15,
Orzola €3.60, Playa Honda €1.40,
Playa Blanca €3.60,
Puerto del Carmen €1.70,
Puerto Calero €1.80,
Teguise €1.40,
Uga €2.00, Yaiza €2.20.

Please have change ready to pay
your fare and avoid using large
Euro notes.

Playa Blanca Bus Station

Major Bus Lines

01 ARRECIFE - COSTA TEGUISE
Approx every 20 minutes weekdays and every 30 minutes at weekends and fiestas.

02 ARRECIFE - PUERTO DEL CARMEN
Approx every 20 minutes weekdays and every 30 minutes at weekends and fiestas.

03 COSTA TEGUISE - PUERTO DEL CARMEN
Approx every 20 minutes weekdays and every 30 minutes at weekends and fiestas.

05 ARRECIFE - FEMÉS
MONDAY TO FRIDAY only (excluding holidays) From Arrecife Bus Station: 08:15 14:10 19:15
From Femés: 09:00 15:00 20:00

07 ARRECIFE - MÁGUEZ
Appox 2 hourly service weekdays and weekends

09 ARRECIFE - ÓRZOLA
Weekdays Arrecife Bus Station: 7:20 10:15 11:30 15:30 17:00 **Órzola:** 8:40 11:40 13.10 16:40 18.10
WeekendsArrecife Bus Station: 7:30 10.15 15:30 17.00 **Órzola:** 8:40 11:40 16:40 18:10

10 ARRECIFE - TEGUISE - LOS VALLES
Weekdays Arrecife Bus Station: 6:10 10:00 14:00 16:00 20:40 **Los Valles:** 6:40 10:30 14:30 16:30 21:10

Sundays only
Costa Teguise: 9:00 9:30 10:00 10:30 11:00 **Teguise market:** 12:00 12:30 13:00 13:15 14:00

Sundays only
Puerto del Carmen 9:00 9:30 10:00 10:30 11:00 **Teguise Market** 12:00 12:30 13:00 13:15 14:00

Sundays only
Playa Blanca 9:00 **Teguise Market** 13:30

Sundays only
Arrecife 7.00 **Teguise Market** 15.30

Weekdays approx hourly from 7:00 until 20:10
Weekends approx two hourly from 8:00 until 20:30

Weekdays
From Arrecife Bus Station: 7:00 8:15 14:00 19:15 **From La Asomada:** 7:30 9:20 15:05 20:20

Weekdays
From Arrecife Bus Station: 6:30 9:45 14:00 17:45 20:45 **From Caleta Famara:** 7:00 10:30 14:45 18:30 21:30

Weekdays
From Arrecife Bus Station: approx every 15-30 mins from 8.10 until 22:50
From Playa Honda: approx every 15-30 mins from 8.25 until 23.05

Weekdays
Arrecife Bus Station to Airport: approx every 25 mins from 7.55 until 22.30
Airport to Arrecife Bus Station: approx every 25 mins from 7.00 until 22.15

Weekends
From Arrecife Bus Station to Airport: approx every 50 mins from 7.00 until 21.00
From Airport to Arrecife Bus Station: approx every 50 mins from 7.10 until 20.20

Weekdays
From Alonso, Arrecife to Puerto Calero: 7:00 9:00 11:20 15:00 19:40 23:20
From Puerto Calero to Alonso, Arrecife: 7:30 9:30 11:50 15:30 20:10 24:00
Weekends
From Alonso, Arrecife to Puerto Calero: 7:20 10:20 11:50 14:50 19:50 23:20
From Puerto Calero to Alonso, Arrecife: 7:50 10:50 12:20 15:20 20:20 24:00

Weekdays
From Arrecife Bus Station to Yé: 18:30 **From Yé to Arrecife Bus Station:** 6:50

Playa Blanca Bus Station - Sun Beach - C C Papagayo - Princesa Yaiza - Castillo del Aguila - Ciudad Jardin 2 - San Marcial 2 - Las Coloradas - San Marcial 1 - Marina Rubicón - Playa Dorada - Lanzarote Princess - Playa Blanca port) - Flamingo - Volcanes 2 - Volcanes 1 - Natura Palace - Rubicón Palace - La Goleta 2 - Faro Park - Los Arcos - Bajo Los Riscos - Jardin del Sol - Virginia Park - El Pueblito - Collegio - La Perla 1 - Las Margaritas - Playa Limones - Casas del Sol - Playa Blanca Bus Station
Daily Service approx every 30 mins from 6:30 until 22:00

Weekdays From Arrecife approx hourly 7:00 until 21:00
From Playa Blanca approx hourly from 8:00 until 22:00
Weekends From Arrecife approx two hourly from 7:00 until 21:00
From Playa Blanca approx two hourly from 8:00 until 22:00

Lanzarote

Tour & Trail

Super-Durable Map

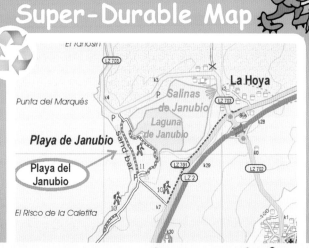

El Janosin
LZ 703
La Hoya
k3
P Salinas
de Janubio
Punta del Marqués
k4
P
Laguna
de Janubio
Playa de Janubio
Playa del
Janubio
El Risco de la Caletita
LZ 703
LZ 701
k29
LZ 702
LZ 2
k7
k30

Super-Durable
Waterproof Map

Cortijo
de la
Mareta
k32

Including GR131 &
Walk Lanzarote Routes
5th Edition

Discovery Walking Guides Ltd
ISBN 9781782750413
Copyright David Brawn 2017

We make no apologies for encouraging you to pair your *Walk! Lanzarote* (4th edition) with our **Lanzarote Tour & Trail Super-Durable Map** (5th edition).

Our new book and map are researched and designed in parallel with the same publication date. There are good, solid, reasons why our book and map are the most poular and most highly reviewed publications for Lanzarote.

Lanzarote Tour & Trail Super-Durable Map
gives you:-
A large 960mm by 700mm double sided map sheet at 40,000 scale,
with a generous common section between NE and SW sides.
the biggest map of the island.
Despite its large size the map is easy to use thanks to our
specialist 'Concertina Map Fold' for easy unfolding,
and, importantly, refolding back to pocket size.

'Super-Durable'
means this map will survive the toughest of adventures.

'2 Year Guarantee'
against splitting or falling apart under adventurous use
DWG are the only publisher to Guarantee their Maps.

'Waterproof'
means you can wipe your map clean with a damp cloth,
and even read it in the shower or the pool.

'Fully Recyclable'
not that you would want to recycle this map

Of course you get our legendary '**Tour & Trail**' level of detail including those all important filling stations, miradors, bar/cafe/restaurants with parking, up to date road numbering, clear road classification, off tarmac details of tracks and trails from our detailed research and 'gps ground survey'.
GR131 (green) and **Walk! Lanzarote** (red) walking routes are clearly highlighted on the map.

at £8.99 this map is reassuringly great value.

Lanzarote Tour & Trail Custom Map
(free download from DWG)

is a digital one-piece version of our printed map at a 240dpi resolutionin kmz file format for viewing using Garmin Basecamp and Google Earth software.
Simply download the Custom Map from our website.
In Garmin Basecamp the digital map will open as a flat sheet in its world location.
In Google Earth the digital map is flowed over GE's 3D terrain mode; very impressive in GE's 'fly-over' view.
Download from Discovery Walking Guides's website Lanzarote webpage at
www.dwgwalking.co.uk

send to David & Ros at **ask.discovery@ntlworld.com**

Updating Notes

send to David & Ros at **ask.discovery@ntlworld.com**

send to David & Ros at **ask.discovery@ntlworld.com**